Contents

Faith and Doubt of John Betjeman

An Anthology of Betjeman's Religious Verse

Edited and introduced by
Kevin J. Gardner

continuum

Continuum
The Tower Building
11 York Road
London SE1 7NX

15 East 26th Street
New York
NY 10010

www.continuumbooks.com

First published 2005

British Library Cataloguing-in-Publication Data
A catalogue record for this book is available from the British Library.

ISBN: 0–8264–8578–2

Typeset by Free Range Book Design & Production
Printed and bound in Great Britain by MPG Books Ltd, Bodmin, Cornwall

Preface

Sir John Betjeman was one of the most remarkable men of the twentieth century. Poet laureate, architectural critic and defender of England's heritage, a man of boundless energy and talent, Betjeman was a generous and committed friend to countless people and to the nation, and his life has now been remembered in Bevis Hillier's magisterial biographical triptych.[1] Even 20 years after his death, many people still have a vivid memory of Betjeman: perhaps as the poet of suburbia, or as the beloved teddy bear to a nation, or as the devotee of causes that at one time must have seemed amusingly quaint or even eccentric. City churches, Victorian railway stations, gas lamps and the Metroland were among the threatened hallmarks of English culture whose preservation he pioneered. John Betjeman was, moreover, a complex of contradictions: a retiring poet who enjoyed being a public figure; a lover of steam engines and all things archaic who adroitly used radio and television to advance his causes; a lifelong Anglican and preserver of churches who struggled mightily to believe the faith.

It is the aspect of Betjeman and his religion that is the occasion of this book. As the great poet of the Church of England in the twentieth century, Betjeman used his astonishing talent for poetry to show us how to think about Anglicanism, about the Church of England and about Christianity in general. Betjeman in fact wrote dozens of poems directly on ecclesial and religious

---

[1] Bevis Hillier, *Young Betjeman* (London: John Murray, 1988); *John Betjeman: New Fame, New Love* (London: John Murray, 2002); *John Betjeman: The Bonus of Laughter* (London: John Murray, 2004).

themes, many of them not normally anthologized. His poems describe the perils of faith and the struggle to believe; they celebrate the social and cultural significance of the Church of England; they reveal the intersection of architecture and faith, of aesthetics and the spirit; and they also demonstrate the social and spiritual failure of the church, particularly the vanity and hypocrisy of its clergy and parishioners. Whether his poems celebrate or satirize, it is clear that Betjeman loved his church and celebrated its role in providing a cultural identity for the English people.

It is the remarkable fact of Betjeman's studied faith in an age of scepticism, his tenderness in a time of jaundiced cynicism, that makes him interesting and worthy of attention. Betjeman could be a brilliant ironist, but he could also be sentimental about the Church of England, and even though he was never an unabashed apologist for his church, his rejection of scepticism has been perceived by some critics as an intellectual weakness. Perhaps this is because he rejected other trends of modernism as well; his sense of poetic tradition is evident in the apparent simplicity of his poems and in his appeals to the experiences and tastes of the common Englishman. That his poems seem to capture so accurately and emotionally what it means to be English and to live in England may best account for the enduring popularity of his verse. As Philip Larkin wrote:

> Betjeman's poems would be something I should want to take with me if I were a soldier leaving England: I can't think of any other poet who has preserved so much of what I should want to remember, nor one who, to use his own words, would so easily suggest 'It is those we are fighting for, foremost of all.' [1]

---

[1]   Philip Larkin, *Required Writing: Miscellaneous Poems 1955–1982* (New York: Farrer Strauss Giroux, 1983), p. 214.

Betjeman is one of the most accessible of all modern poets; his poetry is 'easy' to read, but rejects easy, simplistic notions, instead embracing tremendous profundities about matters of the spirit. It is Betjeman's nature as a poet of faith that is the theme for this volume of his poetry.

For this edition of Betjeman's poetry I have many people to thank. I am immensely grateful to the estate of the late Sir John Betjeman and to his publishers at John Murray for the opportunity to edit and publish this collection of his poetry. I owe my editor at Continuum, Robin Baird-Smith, a debt of gratitude for his tireless championing of this project and his patient guidance of it past many hurdles. Also assisting in this project at Continuum were Ben Hayes, Andrew Walby, Anya Wilson, Margaret Wallis and Jane Boughton. For the editorial aid of Sabahat Jahan, Justin Raab and Jayne Lawrence, my research assistants at Baylor University, I am deeply appreciative as well. It was while teaching a class on Betjeman at my parish that I developed the idea for this book, so I must thank a group of my fellow parishioners at St Paul's Episcopal Church for sharing my enthusiasm for Betjeman and for encouraging me to edit and publish this volume. Finally, it is my great good fortune to have the enduring love and encouragement of my wife, Hilary, and son, Graham. To them I am profoundly grateful, and to them I dedicate this book.

Kevin J. Gardner
Waco, Texas, November 2004

There lives more faith in honest doubt,
Believe me, than in half the creeds.

(Tennyson, *In Memoriam*)

Introduction

In a letter written on Christmas Day, 1947, John Betjeman confessed Christianity's influence on his poetry:

> Also my view of the world is that man is born to fulfil the purposes of his Creator, i.e. to Praise his Creator, to stand in awe of Him and to dread Him. In this way I differ from most modern poets, who are agnostics and have an idea that Man is the centre of the Universe or is a helpless bubble blown about by uncontrolled forces.[1]

Indeed, John Betjeman was one of the more significant literary figures of our time openly to declare his Christian faith and to use his formidable poetic gifts to address issues of personal faith and institutional religion at length. The range of what Betjeman had to say about the Church is quite broad indeed. He wrote of the beauty of the Church, of the joy of its liturgy and worship, of the Church's role in providing cultural identity for the English people. However, he was never a simple apologist for the Church or for Christianity. He wrote scathingly and satirically of ecclesiastical and spiritual corruption, smugness and complacency. He posed questions about faith and the struggle to believe. He described the anxiety of death without the certainty of Christian consolation. And yet, despite such doubts and frustrations, he wrote unapologetically about his faith. He

---

[1] Letter to John Sparrow, in John Betjeman, *Letters (Vol. 1: 1926–51)*, ed. Candida Lycett Green (London: Methuen, 1994), p. 405.

celebrated the mystery of the Eucharist, discovering evidence of the Incarnation all around him in the world.

Perhaps the most distinct recurring image in Betjeman's poetry is that of church bells. The sensual effect of hearing their magnificent pealing is described in 'Church of England Thoughts'. Bells summon the believer to worship, to a communal tradition, to a metaphysical experience of nature and eternity. Alas, they also mocked the poet whose spirit was at times emptied of faith. The church bell was Betjeman's muse; he gave credence to such a notion by titling his verse autobiography, an account of his poetic and spiritual awakening, *Summoned by Bells*.[1] The ringing of church bells gives voice to various ideas of eternity. Throughout his poems Betjeman suggested that a timeless and traditional Anglican worship, embodied in its liturgy, music, bells, stained glass and architecture, is the best means of approximating the eternity of the divine; the best we can do to honour God is to create a living tradition of worship. Yet he also suggested the folly of human endeavour and the futility of our desire to share in God's timelessness: all human action and effort are confounded by our foolish need to control God and time. While some of his poems hint at the wonder of eternity, others deal with the issue of eternity more problematically – namely by exploring the struggle to sustain faith and the uncertainty of eternity beyond the inevitability of death.

Eucharistic and incarnational imagery also predominate in his work. For Betjeman, there may be no stronger statement of his faith in God's real presence and incarnational nature than in the mysterious symbolism of the Eucharist. The Incarnation and the Eucharist together are Betjeman's symbols of the mystery of Christianity. In the midst of normal human triviality appeared God incarnate, at the Nativity, and yet more mysterious is God's immanence today in the metaphysical reality of the eucharistic elements. In his verse, Betjeman revealed his belief

---

[1]   John Betjeman, *Summoned by Bells* (London: John Murray, 1960).

that God remains incarnate in the world all around us: in the Church, in the natural world, in the heart of the believer and even in the life of the doubter. Despite his faith in God's presence in the Eucharist, Betjeman did not attempt to limit encounters with God to experiences that require a priest and the trappings of Anglican worship. God is to be experienced in all things, and may even be discovered in the strangest and unlikeliest of places.

With so much of his verse devoted to his faith and to the spiritual and social roles of the Church of England, it is no surprise that Betjeman's own life was framed by devout observance of Anglican worship. However, faith was not always an easy matter for him. As Auberon Waugh (son of the novelist Evelyn Waugh) wrote, 'I am almost certain he decided to affect a cosy certainty in religion which he was never within miles of feeling.'[1] He was often plagued by nagging spiritual doubts: a fear that he was unfit for heaven, a terror of dying and an anxiety that Christianity's promises might all be empty. Still, he tried to maintain his faith. In 1947 he exchanged a series of letters about faith with Evelyn Waugh, who had recently converted to Roman Catholicism. Betjeman confessed to his old friend that he was 'assailed by doubt', yet he insisted, 'I do know for certain that there is nothing else I want to believe but that Our Lord was the son of God and all He said is true.'[2] Betjeman tried to overcome his spiritual fears by participating in the traditions of Christian worship. As he once wrote in *The Spectator*, 'the only practical way to face the dreaded lonely journey into Eternity seems to me the Christian one. I therefore try to believe that Christ was God, made Man and gives Eternal Life, and that I may be confirmed in this belief by clinging to the sacraments and by prayer.'[3]

---

[1] Auberon Waugh, 'Is Trifle Sufficient?', *The Spectator*, 26 May 1984, p. 6.
[2] In Lycett Green (ed.), *Letters*, vol. 1, p. 405.
[3] John Betjeman, 'John Betjeman Replies,' *The Spectator*, 8 October 1954, p. 443.

Despite his frequent attendance at church and his partaking of the sacrament of the Eucharist, it has often been said – perhaps most famously in a Channel 4 biography, 'The Real John Betjeman' (2000) – that Betjeman could not believe in any aspect of the Church other than the symbolic cohesion it provided the English. Betjeman's own writings reveal that this interpretation of his faith is an overstatement; to Evelyn Waugh he admitted that 'upbringing, habit, environment, connections – all sorts of worldly things – make me love the C of E.' But he went on to insist that those things would not matter at all, 'if I *knew*, in the Pauline sense, that Our Lord was not present at an Anglican Mass'.[1] All his life he had desired to rid himself of uncertainty, but the difficulty in believing persisted. In *Summoned by Bells*, for instance, he recalled sitting in chapel during school at Marlborough and experiencing a deep frustration at the gulf that separates the human and the divine:

> Oh, who is God? O tell me, who is God?
> Perhaps He hides behind the reredos . . .
> Give me a God whom I can touch and see.[2]

The lament Betjeman describes here – a sensation of God's absence – is one that he would voice again and again. Though he loved the Church and its rituals, he often struggled mightily to embrace the central Christian tenets of God's forgiveness and eternal life.

Betjeman's tortuous journey through the Church is worth recounting. This journey is marked by distinct and recurring motifs, the first of which was a regular observance of the sacraments and a devotion to the life of the Church. He was baptized on 25 November 1906 at St Anne Brookfield, a Victorian church near the family home in Parliament Hill Mansions in the north

---

[1]   In Lycett Green (ed.), *Letters*, vol. 1, p. 403.
[2]   Betjeman, *Summoned by Bells*, p. 67.

London suburb of Highgate West Hill. (Betjeman would later recall his Highgate parish church: 'the bells of sad St. Anne's' and the 'awe and mystery ... in the purple dark of thin St. Anne's'.) Following an adolescent affectation of atheism at Marlborough, where he refused the sacrament of confirmation, he was at last confirmed at Oxford's Pusey House when he was an undergraduate at Magdalen. In 1933 he eloped with Penelope Chetwode, the ceremony kept secret in order to postpone the wrath of Penelope's aristocratic father and to prevent her losing her annual allowance. Though the union was sealed in a London register office, at John's insistence the marriage was solemnized afterwards in a nearby church, St Anselm's, Davies Street. Other than a brief period of worshipping with the Quakers in the 1930s, Betjeman made every effort to receive the sacrament of Communion as frequently as possible. And in 1984 he was buried in the churchyard of St Enodoc, near his home in Trebetherick, Cornwall.

In addition to observing the sacraments, Betjeman's religious life was also characterized by an abiding commitment to the life of the Church of England. During his and Penelope's years in Berkshire, and then in London when his work in journalism and broadcasting necessitated that he take a flat in the City, Betjeman was constantly active in a series of parishes. At Uffington St Mary, a church which many architectural critics – including Betjeman – have suggested is the most nearly perfect medieval church in England, he served as people's warden. Here he learned the art of bell-ringing, which would become such an important symbol in his poetry. Also at Uffington John and Penelope organized a parochial youth fellowship, and their efforts, though largely of a secular entertainment nature, were much appreciated by the villagers. At All Saints, Farnborough, where Betjeman is memorialized in a window by John Piper, he saw himself and Penelope as the chief supporters of the parish. In a letter to Evelyn Waugh in 1947 he wrote:

> If we were to desert it, there would be no one to whip up people to attend the services, to run the church organisations, to keep the dilatory and woolly-minded incumbent (who lives in another village) to the celebration of Communion services any Sunday. It is just because it is so disheartening and so difficult and so easy to betray, that we must keep this Christian witness going. In villages people still follow a lead and we are the only people here who will give a lead. I know that to desert this wounded and neglected church would be to betray Our Lord.[1]

Eventually, John was left to lead the parish by himself, as Penelope – partly through the influence of Waugh – renounced Anglicanism in favour of Roman Catholicism. When the family moved to Wantage in 1951, Betjeman was again involved in the parish church. At SS Peter and Paul he served as churchwarden, lent the growing fame of his name to such mundane events as church bazaars and wrote the parish history. When he took up part-time residence in London in 1954, he attended services at St Bartholomew the Great in West Smithfield and served on its parochial church council. There he met the chaplain of St Bartholomew's Hospital, through whose influence he took up a ministry of hospital visitation to terminally ill patients.

Betjeman's ministry to the dying is related to the second motif in his spiritual journey: an anxiety about death. In early childhood, he was much troubled by fears of damnation that would in adulthood be supplanted not so much by a mature confidence in God's grace but by fears of extinction. In 1945 he could be found preferring his childish visions of hell to an eternal nothingness promised by existential philosophers:

> Oh better far those echoing hells
> Half-threaten'd in the pealing bells

---

[1] Lycett Green (ed.), *Letters*, vol. 1, pp. 411–12.

Than that this 'I' should cease to be—
Come quickly, Lord, come quick to me.[1]

He first heard of hell from his 'hateful nurse', Maud; tormented by Calvinistic demons, she was convinced she would be consumed by eternal flames. Her fears taught him to dread God's wrath and to doubt himself – anxieties he was never to outgrow. Despite the psychological torture of this early experience, the young Betjeman embraced the Church, even writing his earliest verses in imitation of the Anglican hymnal, *Hymns Ancient and Modern*.

Indeed, Betjeman continued to be fascinated by the Church and all that went with it. A third motif in his journey appears in his love of the aesthetics of English churches. This began to take hold of him during his prep-school days at the Dragon School, Oxford, where he developed a scholarly knowledge of English ecclesiastical architecture. At weekends, he would cycle round Oxford, carefully exploring its churches and absorbing as much of its history and aesthetics as he could apprehend:

Who knew what undiscovered glories hung
Waiting in locked-up churches—vaulting shafts,
Pillar-piscinas, floriated caps,
Squints, squinches, low side windows, quoins and
groins —
Till I had roused the Vicar, found the key,
And made a quick inspection of the church?[2]

Cursory inspections gave way to detailed examinations as an adult, when Betjeman became well-known for his writings on church architecture, a lifetime pursuit crowned by his *Collins' Guide to English Parish Churches* and the BBC documentary 'A

---

[1] 'Before the Anaesthetic', *New Bats in Old Belfries* (London: John Murray, 1945).
[2] Betjeman, *Summoned by Bells*, p. 48.

Passion for Churches'. Of the two hundred or more civic and ecclesiastical organizations that he served or supported during his lifetime, the diocesan advisory committees of London and Oxford were among his strongest commitments. He served on the Oxford Diocesan Advisory Committee for 32 years as an adviser on matters of ecclesiastical architecture, and he was also active on both the Council for the Care of Churches and the Historic Churches Preservation Trust.

Eventually Betjeman grew to love the ritual of the Church as much as its architecture – a love that was to evolve into the fourth and final motif of his spiritual journey. All things liturgical – aumbry and thurible, cassock and alb, canticle and versicle – appealed deeply to Betjeman's growing fascination with the mystery of the Church of England. One of his favourite boyhood activities was attending services of Evening Prayer on his Sundays in London. In *Summoned by Bells* he fondly describes intentionally seeking out obscure and quiet churches in the City, listening for a single bell, looking for an empty nave – 'St Botolph this, St Mary that'. What drew him to these services was not really faith, however, but 'a longing for the past, / With a slight sense of something unfulfilled'. It would be years before this longing and seeking turned into something more closely resembling mature faith. For the time being, Anglican tradition meant little more to him than English tradition; these City churches embodied England's fading past, to which the budding poet was instinctively drawn.

Betjeman continued his explorations of churches during family seaside holidays in Cornwall. The rector of St Ervan's Church drew his attention from the humble and cosy Evensong to grander notions of Celtic mysticism, which encouraged him to search for the divine in nature. Although 'no mystical experience was vouchsafed' for Betjeman in Cornish holy sites, he continued to seek and to feel, and he often drew upon Celtic mysticism in his poetry. He once averred that his encounter with the priest in St Ervan's was life-changing. If so, it must be that it opened his heart to prepare it for something new and different – something that would make a much greater impact on him than either Celtic mysticism or the familiar language and liturgy of the Anglican Book of Common Prayer.

That something different was Anglo-Catholicism, which he first encountered while a university student at Oxford. High Mass at Pusey House was not merely an aesthetic experience for Betjeman. As he recounts in *Summoned by Bells*, it was also theological. It was not Christian truth that he discovered, however, but the quest for that truth, a quest he would sustain all his life. For Betjeman, Christianity was never merely the trappings of Anglo-Catholicism, yet those elements served as the lintel of his faith:

> The steps to truth were made by sculptured stone,
> Stained glass and vestments, holy-water stoups,
> Incense and crossings of myself—[1]

Although Anglo-Catholicism did provide a theological awakening for Betjeman, it is likely that he remained a little too much attached to the aesthetic experience, for he neglected to apply himself to his studies. When his tutor, the Magdalen don C. S. Lewis, failed him in Divinity, Betjeman left Oxford without a degree.

> Failed in Divinity! Oh count the hours
> Spent on my knees in Cowley, Pusey House,
> St Barnabas', St Mary Mag's, St Paul's,
> Revering chasubles and copes and albs![2]

High Church Anglicanism was to guide Betjeman in the struggles of his faith throughout his adult life. When doubts arose, the timeless permanence of Anglo-Catholicism was a

[1] Ibid., p. 96.
[2] Ibid., p. 106.

reliable support on which to lean. It was a bastion of Anglo-Catholicism that was Betjeman's last church affiliation. In his final years he was a regular member of the congregation at Grosvenor Chapel on South Audley Street in Mayfair; when he grew too frail to attend services, he received Communion from the Revd Gerard Irvine at home in Chelsea, an ironing-board serving as a makeshift altar.

John Betjeman may thus be characterized as a practising Christian who wrestled with matters of faith. His Christian faith was neither smug nor self-assured; in fact, it was riddled with uncertainty and questions. Because of this, he was able to use his gift for poetry to describe not only the arc of his own religious belief but to illumine the nature of faith and doubt for all people. It is perhaps his capacity for doubt that makes Betjeman the great poet of the Church of England in the twentieth century, for faith is deepened by questioning. It is my hope that readers will find in these poems inspiration from an immensely talented poet who wanted to believe – and often did.

1

Spiritual Doubts and Fears

1 Spiritual Doubts and Fears

A recurrent pattern in John Betjeman's poetry is his reflection on guilt, judgement, damnation and death. There are many variations on this motif, but a central element is always there: that neither he himself nor God nor the Church can save him from his emotional and spiritual torment, whether the torment is a fear of hell's flames or the anxiety of extinction into nothingness. As Betjeman reflected through poetry on his life, he found these doubts and fears both in his adult experiences and in his early childhood memories.

'N.W.5 & N.6' (the title alludes to the postal codes of the north London suburbs of Betjeman's very early childhood) reveals that Betjeman's spiritual fears were instilled in him by his nanny. Her tales of the gaping maw of hell, licking its chops in anticipation of her own certain and imminent arrival, were sufficient to plant an ineradicable anxiety in his mind, although she never suggested that he too was destined for this fate. His childhood misunderstanding made 'World without end' (a phrase from the *Gloria patri* that follows the psalm and canticles in the Anglican services of Morning and Evening Prayer) not a promise of eternal bliss for those of Christian hope but a threat of certain eternal damnation for children everywhere.

Two of Betjeman's poems explore the effects of the Calvinistic theology that produced the mindset of the nanny whose tales had so terrified him as a child. In 'Calvinistic Evensong' Betjeman imagines eavesdropping on Evensong in an Anglican parish stricken and withered by Calvinism with a congregation decayed into six elderly women and a sinister curate. Imagery of death pervades the poem: the minister preaches on death; the parish itself, shrivelling in numbers, begins to reek of decay; and the trees in the churchyard are hungry for their next feeding of parishioners' bodies. The fruit of Calvinism, Betjeman suggests, is a miserable life spent fearing death, followed by the miserable fulfilment of that anxiety. If the poem contains a dark sense of graveyard humour, it is because Betjeman could find a temporary solace from this same anxiety by laughing grimly at it. 'Matlock Bath' shows the poet walking in the eponymous Derbyshire town and listening to the hymn-singing of a Nonconformist congregation, echoes of whose hymns fill the lines of the poem. Ultimately the Calvinistic hymns he hears burden him with anxiety of falling into damnation. He tries to mask this spiritual fear of falling behind the physical fear of slipping into the River Derwent below him, but his real dread – misinterpreting the message as he did with 'World without end' – is that the Rock of Ages will swallow him into an eternal doom. This misinterpretation arises at least in part because he chooses to view the rock and the water with fear and because he equates these symbols with other childhood anxieties. The numerous images of water seem to admit the possibility of baptismal regeneration, but his fear of the water and of submersion into God implies his inability to embrace this form of spiritual union.

'Original Sin on the Sussex Coast', like 'N.W.5 & N.6', is constructed around Proustian memories as the adult Betjeman is led by sensory impressions into the recollection of a painful childhood experience of bullying. Being beaten up by other children is for Betjeman no mere rite of passage but evidence of a central tenet of Christian doctrine. Not only does the title supply this interpretation, however. Mum can launder her bullying son's clothes with Persil, but she can't scrub clean his soul from original sin. The contrast between the boys' actions and appearances reveals the darkness we all hide in our souls, symbolized by the falling light Betjeman describes in the poem:

outwardly we are like the boys with their innocent satchels of homework heading happily home for a snack of Post-Toasties, but the encroaching darkness of the sunset on the Sussex Downs hides our lurking sins.

In 'Norfolk', Betjeman laments the inevitable loss of childhood innocence while suggesting that this loss has a theological explanation. With echoes of Blake, he juxtaposes images of innocence and experience onto a memory of a barge holiday with his father along the River Bure in Norfolk. The obscure allusion to Fowler of Louth implies an analogy between church restoration and our psychological efforts to restore ourselves to some version of childhood innocence. Betjeman's implication seems to be that since we will inevitably fail at restoring our own innocence (as Fowler surely failed in the eyes of Betjeman, the architectural critic and purist), only God can effect our restoration. However, most people are fooled by Fowler's work – and by themselves, blinding themselves to the failure of their own self-restorations. The poem concludes with something like a prayer: Betjeman petitions time to restore the rapturous ignorance of long ago, an apparent plea for prelapsarian innocence and grace.

The tenderness for his father in this memory is unusual. More common is the fear of parental judgement and wrath that Betjeman describes in 'Narcissus' and 'Archibald', two poems that focus on the overwhelming sense of personal shame and worthlessness that accompanies his sense of spiritual doom. 'Narcissus' presents us with the perspectives of both adulthood and childhood on the painful experience of his forced separation from a treasured friend. As a child, Betjeman suffered confusion over this separation and a desire to do anything to be restored to his friend. The adult Betjeman has come to understand that he had been engaging in inappropriate sexual exploration. Notably, his mother reinforces the fear that he is doomed to hell, while Archibald, his teddy-bear, remains his sole comfort. The poem 'Archibald' further explores the comfort of a childhood toy in a house of isolation and anger. As if embarrassed by his attachment to the bear, Betjeman begins the poem with light, rollicking rhythms that undermine the bear's apparent evangelical fervour and doomsday judgement. The poem quickly turns serious, however, as it begins to explore traumatic memories of childhood. The sight of the bear which he has kept all these years fills him with a sense of dread and despair that are adult enhancements of his childhood anxieties. The harsh and judgemental voices of his parents are transferred to the bear, which he now imagines telling him he is going to hell; still he cannot part with the toy. Despite the bear's mockery of his immortal soul, to contemplate its loss is to contemplate venturing into a void of darkness and emptiness.

This fear of a spiritual void points to the central theological dilemma in 'Before the Anaesthetic', one of Betjeman's greatest poems. Here, he describes the tremendous efforts he has taken to assure himself an eternity in heaven; however, despite every effort to believe and to worship, at this moment God is only an illusion. Throughout the poem we hear the ringing of the bells of St Giles's, but their empty peals fill the poet with horror at the absence of God. The great fear he then expresses is not hell but extinction; ironically, having given up hope in heavenly bliss, he finds himself wishing for the flames of hell as opposed to the alternative of nothingness. To Betjeman, at least hell is a kind of eternity – and perhaps an affirmation, however unfortunate, that all his efforts to worship and believe, however ineffectual, were not misguided and incorrect. To end up in hell would at least prove to him that he was right in trying to believe. Betjeman once expressed this sentiment in an interview with Alan Neame, asserting that 'I'd rather Hell than Nothing!'[1] Although his preference for hell over oblivion was surely hyperbolic, it illustrates Betjeman's desperation for any assurance of eternal life.

---

[1]   Alan Neame, 'Poet of Anglicanism', *Commonweal* 71 (4 December 1959), p. 283.

The failure of the Church to provide Betjeman with a sense of spiritual security is a central theme in several poems. 'Goodbye' and 'Fruit' both reveal the tiniest measure of acceptance in his mind of the likelihood of death bringing oblivion. It is no happy thought, but it is one he has no energy to oppose, and he finds a passive acquiescence in having merely struggled to live and accomplish a few small achievements. 'On Leaving Wantage 1972' begins with an optimistic image of the struggle of the Church to unite humanity in the symbolic act of bell-ringing, but Betjeman concludes with an image of the implacable force of time sweeping all things away. 'Loneliness' likewise suggests that religion is only a tonic to fortify the believer against the fear of death. Subverting the usual associations of spring and rebirth with Easter, Betjeman describes the ringing of Easter bells amidst the bleakness of late winter's cold air, blackened branches and withered leaves. Even the very earliest signs of spring mock the illusion of rebirth, as Betjeman uses the metaphor of spring growth as a tumour to suggest an analogy that comprises the poem's theme: that the rituals we use to mask the ugly reality of death remind us that the rituals of religion mask man's isolation in creation. 'Aldershot Crematorium' also describes how institutional religion offers cold comfort for the grieving. The dead are not resurrected, though cremation provides a symbolic, heavenward gesture. The image of the dead wafting skyward into nothingness mocks the poet's notions of Christ's ascension and the promise of eternal life. In all these poems, the consolations of Christianity seem to be no more than empty words blowing in the wind.

N.W.5 & N.6

Red cliffs arise. And up them service lifts
   Soar with the groceries to silver heights.
Lissenden Mansions. And my memory sifts
   Lilies from lily-like electric lights
And Irish-stew smells from the smell of prams
And roar of seas from roar of London trams.

Out of it all my memory carves the quiet
   Of that dark privet hedge where pleasures breed,
There first, intent upon its leafy diet,
   I watched the looping caterpillar feed
And saw it hanging in a gummy froth
Till, weeks on, from the chrysalis burst the moth.

I see black oak twigs outlined on the sky,
   Red squirrels on the Burdett-Coutts[1] estate.
I ask my nurse the question 'Will I die?'
   As bells from sad St Anne's[2] ring out so late,
'And if I do die, will I go to Heaven?'
Highgate at eventide. Nineteen-eleven.

'You will. I won't.' From that cheap nursery-maid,
   Sadist and puritan as now I see,
I first learned what it was to be afraid,
   Forcibly fed when sprawled across her knee
Lock'd into cupboards, left alone all day,
'World without end.' What fearsome words to pray.

---

[1] Baroness Angela Burdett-Coutts (1814–1906) was a nineteenth-century heiress whose many philanthropic schemes included providing a home for prostitutes and housing estates for the working class.

[2] Betjeman was baptized in the church of St Anne Brookfield on 25 November 1906.

'World without end.' It was not what she'ld do
   That frightened me so much as did her fear
And guilt at endlessness. I caught them too,
   Hating to think of sphere succeeding sphere
Into eternity and God's dread will.
I caught her terror then. I have it still.

Calvinistic Evensong

The six bells stopped, and in the dark I heard
Cold silence wait the Calvinistic word;
For Calvin now the soft oil lamps are lit
Hands on their hymnals six old women sit.
Black gowned and sinister, he now appears
Curate-in-charge of aged parish fears.
Let, unaccompanied, that psalm begin
Which deals most harshly with the fruits of sin!
Boy! pump the organ! let the anthem flow
With promise for the chosen saints below!
Pregnant with warning the globed elm trees wait
Fresh coffin-wood beside the churchyard gate.
And that mauve hat three cherries decorate
Next week shall topple from its trembling perch
While wet fields reek like some long empty church.

Matlock Bath

From Matlock Bath's half-timbered station
    I see the black dissenting spire—
Thin witness of a congregation,
    Stone emblem of a Handel choir;
In blest Bethesda's limpid pool
Comes treacling out of Sunday School.

By cool Siloam's shady rill—
    The sounds are sweet as strawberry jam:
I raise mine eyes unto the hill,
    The beetling HEIGHTS OF ABRAHAM;
The branchy trees are white with rime
In Matlock Bath this winter-time,

And from the whiteness, grey uprearing,
    Huge cliffs hang sunless ere they fall,
A tossed and stony ocean nearing
    The moment to o'erwhelm us all:
Eternal Father, strong to save,
How long wilt thou suspend the wave?

How long before the pleasant acres
    Of intersecting LOVERS' WALKS
Are rolled across by limestone breakers,
    Whole woodlands snapp'd like cabbage stalks?
O God, our help in ages past,
How long will SPEEDWELL CAVERN last?

In this dark dale I hear the thunder
    Of houses folding with the shocks,
The GRAND PAVILION buckling under
    The weight of the ROMANTIC ROCKS,
The hardest Blue John[1] ash-trays seem
To melt away in thermal steam.

Deep in their Nonconformist setting
    The shivering children wait their doom—
The father's whip, the mother's petting
    In many a coffee-coloured room;
And attic bedrooms shriek with fright,
For dread of *Pilgrims of the Night*.

Perhaps it's this that makes me shiver
    As I ascend the slippery path
High, high above the sliding river
    And terraces of Matlock Bath:
A sense of doom, a dread to see
The *Rock of Ages cleft for me*.

---

[1] Blue John is a fluorspar found only in Castleton, Derbyshire, and is said to be the rarest mineral formation in Britain. Blue John craftsmen have produced lovely ornamental and decorative arts since the late nineteenth century.

Original Sin on the Sussex Coast

Now on this out of season afternoon
Day schools which cater for the sort of boy
Whose parents go by Pullman once a month
To do a show in town, pour out their young
Into the sharply red October light.
Here where The Drive and Buckhurst Road converge
I watch the rival gangs and am myself
A schoolboy once again in shivering shorts.
I see the dust of sherbet on the chin
Of Andrew Knox well-dress'd, well-born, well-fed,
Even at nine a perfect gentleman,
Willie Buchanan waiting at his side—
Another Scot, eruptions on his skin.
I hear Jack Drayton whistling from the fence
Which hides the copper domes of 'Cooch Behar'.[1]
That was the signal. So there's no escape.
A race for Willow Way and jump the hedge
Behind the Granville Bowling Club? Too late.
They'll catch me coming out in Seapink Lane.
Across the Garden of Remembrance? No,
That would be blasphemy and bring bad luck.
Well then, I'm *for* it. Andrew's at me first,
He pinions me in that especial grip
His brother learned in Kobë from a Jap
(No chance for me against the Japanese).
Willie arrives and winds me with a punch
Plum in the tummy, grips the other arm.
'You're to be booted. Hold him steady, chaps!'
A wait for taking aim. Oh trees and sky!

---

[1]   Architectural features redolent of the palaces of the Indian maharajahs who ruled the principality of Bengal.

Then crack against the column of my spine,
Blackness and breathlessness and sick with pain
I stumble on the asphalt. Off they go
Away, away, thank God, and out of sight
So that I lie quite still and climb to sense
Too out of breath and strength to make a sound.
    Now over Polegate vastly sets the sun;
Dark rise the Downs from darker looking elms,
And out of Southern Railway trains to tea
Run happy boys down various Station Roads,
Satchels of homework jogging on their backs,
So trivial and so healthy in the shade
Of these enormous Downs. And when they're home,
When the Post-Toasties mixed with Golden Shred
Make for the kiddies such a scrumptious feast,
Does Mum, the Persil-user, still believe
That there's no Devil and that youth is bliss?
As certain as the sun behind the Downs
And quite as plain to see, the Devil walks.

Norfolk

How did the Devil come? When first attack?
　　These Norfolk lanes recall lost innocence,
The years fall off and find me walking back
　　Dragging a stick along the wooden fence
Down this same path, where, forty years ago,
My father strolled behind me, calm and slow.

I used to fill my hand with sorrel seeds
　　And shower him with them from the tops of stiles,
I used to butt my head into his tweeds
　　To make him hurry down those languorous miles
Of ash and alder-shaded lanes, till here
Our moorings and the masthead would appear.

There after supper lit by lantern light
　　Warm in the cabin I could lie secure
And hear against the polished sides at night
　　The lap lap lapping of the weedy Bure,
A whispering and watery Norfolk sound
Telling of all the moonlit reeds around.

How did the Devil come? When first attack?
　　The church is just the same, though now I know
Fowler of Louth[1] restored it. Time, bring back
　　The rapturous ignorance of long ago,
The peace, before the dreadful daylight starts,
Of unkept promises and broken hearts.

---

[1]　James Fowler (1828–92) of Louth, Lincolnshire, was an architect whose excessive restorations Betjeman loathed.

Narcissus

Yes, it was Bedford Park the vision came from—
    de Morgan[1] lustre glowing round the hearth,
And that sweet flower which self-love takes its name from
    Nodding among the lilies in the garth,
And Arnold Dolmetsch[2] touching the spinet,
And Mother, Chiswick's earliest suffragette.

I was a delicate boy—my parents' only—
    And highly strung. My father was in trade.
And how I loved, when Mother left me lonely,
    To watch old Martha spice the marmalade,
Or help with flower arrangements in the lobby
Before I went to find my playmate Bobby.

We'ld go for walks, we bosom boyfriends would
    (For Bobby's watching sisters drove us mad),
And when we just did nothing we were good,
    But when we touched each other we were bad.
I found this out when Mother said one day
She thought we were unwholesome in our play.

So Bobby and I were parted. Bobby dear,
    I didn't want my tea. I heard your sisters
Playing at hide-and-seek with you quite near
    As off the garden gate I picked the blisters.
Oh tell me, Mother, what I mustn't do—
Then, Bobby, I can play again with you.

---

[1] William de Morgan (1839–1917) was the greatest tile and pottery designer of the Arts
and Crafts movement. He was a disciple of William Morris.
[2] Arnold Dolmetsch (1858–1940), of Swiss–French extraction, moved to London
and made a career in the study and promotion of early music and instruments and
of historically sensitive performances.

For I know hide-and-seek's most secret places
　　More than your sisters do. And you and I
Can scramble into them and leave no traces,
　　Nothing above us but the twigs and sky,
Nothing below us but the leaf-mould chilly
Where we can warm and hug each other silly.

My Mother wouldn't tell me why she hated
　　The things we did, and why they pained her so.
She said a fate far worse than death awaited
　　People who did the things we didn't know,
And then she said I was her precious child,
And once there was a man called Oscar Wilde.

'Open your story book and find a tale
　　Of ladyes fayre and deeds of derring-do,
Or good Sir Gawaine and the Holy Grail,
　　Mother will read her boy a page or two
Before she goes, this Women's Suffrage Week,
To hear that clever Mrs Pankhurst[1] speak.

Sleep with your hands above your head. That's right—
　　And let no evil thoughts pollute the dark.'
She rose, and lowered the incandescent light.
　　I heard her footsteps die down Bedford Park.
Mother where are you? Bobby, Bobby, where?
I clung for safety to my teddy bear.

---

[1] Emmeline Pankhurst (1858–1928), with her daughter Christabel, founded the militant Women's Social and Political Union, which fought for women's suffrage.

Archibald[1]

The bear who sits above my bed
    A doleful bear he is to see;
From out his drooping pear-shaped head
    His woollen eyes look into me.
He has no mouth, but seems to say:
'They'll burn you on the Judgment Day.'

Those woollen eyes, the things they've seen
    Those flannel ears, the things they've heard—
Among horse-chestnut fans of green,
    The fluting of an April bird,
And quarrelling downstairs until
Doors slammed at Thirty One West Hill.

The dreaded evening keyhole scratch
    Announcing some return below,
The nursery landing's lifted latch,
    The punishment to undergo—
Still I could smooth those half-moon ears
And wet that forehead with my tears.

Whatever rush to catch a train,
    Whatever joy there was to share
Of sounding sea-board, rainbowed rain,
    Or seaweed-scented Cornish air,
Sharing the laughs, you still were there,
You ugly, unrepentant bear.

---

[1] The bear's full name was Archibald Ormsby-Gore. He features in a book which
Betjeman wrote for his children, *Archie and the Strict Baptists*, illus. Phillida Gili
(London: John Murray, 1977).

When nine, I hid you in a loft
    And dared not let you share my bed;
My father would have thought me soft,
    Or so at least my mother said.
She only then our secret knew,
And thus my guilty passion grew.

The bear who sits above my bed
    More agèd now he is to see,
His woollen eyes have thinner thread,
    But still he seems to say to me,
In double-doom notes, like a knell:
'You're half a century nearer Hell.'

Self-pity shrouds me in a mist,
    And drowns me in my self-esteem.
The freckled faces I have kissed
    Float by me in a guilty dream.
The only constant, sitting there,
Patient and hairless, is a bear.

And if an analyst one day
    Of school of Adler, Jung or Freud
Should take this aged bear away,
    Then, oh my God, the dreadful void!
Its draughty darkness could but be
Eternity, Eternity.

Before the Anaesthetic

Intolerably sad, profound
St Giles's bells are ringing round,[1]
They bring the slanting summer rain
To tap the chestnut boughs again
Whose shadowy cave of rainy leaves
The gusty belfry-song receives.
Intolerably sad and true,
Victorian red and jewel blue,
The mellow bells are ringing round
And charge the evening light with sound,
And I look motionless from bed
On heavy trees and purple red
And hear the midland bricks and tiles
Throw back the bells of stone St Giles,
Bells, ancient now as castle walls,
Now hard and new as pitchpine stalls,
Now full with help from ages past,
Now dull with death and hell at last.
Swing up! and give me hope of life,
Swing down! and plunge the surgeon's knife.
I, breathing for a moment, see
Death wing himself away from me
And think, as on this bed I lie,
Is it extinction when I die?
I move my limbs and use my sight;
Not yet, thank God, not yet the Night.
Oh better far those echoing hells
Half-threaten'd in the pealing bells
Than that this 'I' should cease to be—

[1] The bells of St Giles's, Oxford, have long been famous for their rich beauty and for
the skill of their campanologists.

Come quickly, Lord, come quick to me.
St Giles's bells are asking now
'And hast thou known the Lord, hast thou?'
St Giles's bells, they richly ring
'And was that Lord our Christ the King?'
St Giles's bells they hear me call
I never knew the Lord at all.
Oh not in me your Saviour dwells
You ancient, rich St Giles's bells.
Illuminated missals—spires—
Wide screens and decorated quires—
All these I loved, and on my knees
I thanked myself for knowing these
And watched the morning sunlight pass
Through richly stained Victorian glass
And in the colour-shafted air
I, kneeling, thought the Lord was there.
Now, lying in the gathering mist
I know that Lord did not exist;
Now, lest this 'I' should cease to be,
Come, real Lord, come quick to me.
With every gust the chestnut sighs,
With every breath, a mortal dies;
The man who smiled alone, alone,
And went his journey on his own
With 'Will you give my wife this letter,
In case, of course, I don't get better?'
Waits for his coffin lid to close
On waxen head and yellow toes.
Almighty Saviour, had I Faith
There'd be no fight with kindly Death.
Intolerably long and deep
St Giles's bells swing on in sleep:
'But still you go from here alone'
Say all the bells about the Throne.

Goodbye

Some days before death
   When food's tasting sour on my tongue,
Cigarettes long abandoned,
   Disgusting now even champagne;
When I'm sweating a lot
   From the strain on a last bit of lung
And lust has gone out
   Leaving only the things of the brain;
More worthless than ever
   Will seem all the songs I have sung,
More harmless the prods of the prigs,
   Remoter the pain,
More futile the Lord Civil Servant
   As, rung upon rung,
He ascends by committees to roofs
   Far below on the plain.
But better down there in the battle
   Than here on the hill
With Judgement or nothingness waiting me,
   Lonely and chill.

Fruit

Now with the threat growing still greater within me,
   The Church dead that was hopelessly over-restored,
The fruit picked from these yellowing Worcestershire orchards
   What is left to me, Lord?

To wait until next year's bloom at the end of the garden
   Foams to the Malvern Hills, like an inland sea,
And to know that its fruit, dropping in autumn stillness,
   May have outlived me.

On Leaving Wantage 1972

I like the way these old brick garden walls
Unevenly run down to Letcombe Brook.
I like the mist of green about the elms
In earliest leaf-time. More intensely green
The duck-weed undulates; a mud-grey trout
Hovers and darts away at my approach.

    From rumpled beds on far-off new estates,
From houses over shops along the square,
From red-brick villas somewhat further out,
Ringers arrive, converging on the tower.
    Third Sunday after Easter. Public ways
Reek faintly yet of last night's fish and chips.
The plumes of smoke from upright chimney-pots
Denote the death of last week's Sunday press,
While this week's waits on many a step and sill
Unopened, folded, supplements and all.

    Suddenly on the unsuspecting air
The bells clash out. It seems a miracle
That leaf and flower should never even stir
In such great waves of medieval sound:
They ripple over roofs to fields and farms
So that 'the fellowship of Christ's religion'
Is roused to breakfast, church or sleep again.

    From this wide vale, where all our married lives
We two have lived, we now are whirled away
Momently clinging to the things we knew—
Friends, footpaths, hedges, house and animals—
Till, borne along like twigs and bits of straw,
We sink below the sliding stream of time.

Loneliness

The last year's leaves are on the beech:
    The twigs are black; the cold is dry;
To deeps beyond the deepest reach
    The Easter bells enlarge the sky.
Oh! ordered metal clatter-clang!
Is yours the song the angels sang?
You fill my heart with joy and grief—
Belief! Belief! And unbelief . . .
    And, though you tell me I shall die,
    You say not how or when or why.

Indifferent the finches sing,
    Unheeding roll the lorries past:
What misery will this year bring
    Now spring is in the air at last?
For, sure as blackthorn bursts to snow,
Cancer in some of us will grow,
The tasteful crematorium door
Shuts out for some the furnace roar;
    But church-bells open on the blast
    Our loneliness, so long and vast.

Aldershot Crematorium

Between the swimming-pool and cricket-ground
    How straight the crematorium driveway lies!
And little puffs of smoke without a sound
    Show what we loved dissolving in the skies,
Dear hands and feet and laughter-lighted face
And silk that hinted at the body's grace.

But no one seems to know quite what to say
    (Friends are so altered by the passing years):
'Well, anyhow, it's not so cold today'—
    And thus we try to dissipate our fears.
'I am the Resurrection and the Life':
Strong, deep and painful, doubt inserts the knife.

2

Death

2 Death

A natural connection exists between the measure of Betjeman's spiritual doubts and his views on death. Poems such as 'Before the Anaesthetic' and 'Aldershot Crematorium', which treat death with fear and uncertainty, actually have less to say about death than about his anxiety concerning eternity. This chapter gathers together poems that treat death without substantial reference to matters of faith. 'For Nineteenth-Century Burials' typifies the way Betjeman was at various times able to consider death as a simple finality. This poem touches gently on death's inevitability and passes lovingly over archaic death rituals in Victorian culture. In all of the poems – some of which are more personal and introspective than others – death is considered in non-religious terms; where religion manifests itself in these poems it can be generally dismissed as having no serious emotional hold upon the poet. Other emotional effects of death preoccupy him here; these range from grief, to guilt, to placid acceptance, to emptiness and even to banality.

Betjeman portrays death in several poems as a mundane and ordinary event, part of mundane and ordinary lives. In 'Devonshire Street W.1' an elderly couple leaves a hospital with the dreadful news of a terminal diagnosis. The setting in an elegant Edwardian street contrasts the ugly reality of the husband's death sentence. The wife's consolation is at once human and tender as she slips her fingers into her husband's. The mundanity of death is emphasized as she tries to work out the easiest route home. 'Death in Leamington' sets the mundanity of death within the loneliness of life. An elderly

woman has died alone in a decaying house; her nurse comes in
with a tea tray, discovers she has died, and matter-of-factly
tidies up the medicine bottles before turning down the heat
and leaving the room in an appropriate chill and darkness. The
only beauty is the evening star shining in the bedroom window,
but that light is unfathomably remote, its intensity softened by
the cheap plate-glass window. 'The Cottage Hospital' portrays
the onset of death with equal insignificance, though from a
strikingly different perspective. Here the poet contemplates his
own death as he tries to relax outdoors on a late summer
Sunday. While children play, a fly is trapped in a web and eaten
by a spider. The innocuous events of the day fill the poet with
an arresting sense of the banality of death. Insects buzz, children
play and death slips in. The concluding stanza of the poem
reveals Betjeman imagining his own death rather like the fly's:
unnoticed, insignificant and void of meaning.

Betjeman has a knack for describing death in coldly objective,
if not entirely callous, terms. While the first four poems in this
group examine the creep of death, the next three show death's
aftermath. With a sort of prying, journalistic nosiness Betjeman
imagines what goes on around a life that has ceased to be. It is
as if the dead still have some measure of being, a kind of
emptiness or void around which the survivors must navigate
carefully. The hole does not disappear right away, and it cannot
be ignored. In 'House of Rest' an elderly woman contemplates
the recent death of her husband, a vicar, and the long-ago death
of her sons. She invites the poet, who appears to be visiting her
in a nursing home, to share their living presence in photographs,
memories and such seemingly mundane objects as her husband's
tobacco jar. What becomes of the dead? The vicar is gone, but
not gone: a paradox symbolized by the tobacco jar now filled
with lavender. Betjeman describes, movingly, how at the
Eucharist, the woman is reunited with her family. The veil
dividing her from her loved ones is lifted, and they are drawn
together. He uses the metaphor of the sun struggling to penetrate

the morning mist as a symbol of his own struggle with faith and doubt. 'Variations on a Theme by T. W. Rolleston' also explores this paradox. A mother has died. She is clearly gone, and most of the world is as oblivious to her absence as to her presence. Betjeman's exploration of the significance of her loss is curiously not from the perspective of her loved ones but from that of shopkeepers and bureaucrats. Cobblers and grocers who hardly knew her wonder why she no longer comes to their shops, while civil servants obligingly organize her various documents and close her file with a frightening finality. 'Variation on a Theme by Newbolt' similarly describes the inescapable presence of the dead; our attention is drawn to City boardrooms and clubs, the golf course, and other public spaces where this man passed the moiety of his life. The poem's speaker is a business associate preoccupied with the business of grief rather than by real sorrow. For the most part, he utters the sentiments appropriate to the occasion, but the final stanza lifts us from the banality of death as the speaker contemplates the pain of the lonely and isolated widow.

Not all of Betjeman's poems on death are so objective and remote. He was also capable of imagining death in much more personal terms, and when he does so his own sense of grief becomes clearly apparent. 'I. M. Walter Ramsden' eulogizes an Oxford don, but Betjeman emphasizes not so much Ramsden's achievements or his survivors' memories of him but the sensory associations arising subconsciously along with a contemplation of the deceased – ivy-twined panes, shadows from chimney pots, bees buzzing around window boxes – and the emotions that they evoke. Here death is natural if still mundane, but it is accompanied by a sense of loss and a hint of sorrow. In 'Inevitable' – inspired by his experiences visiting terminally ill patients in St Bartholomew's Hospital – Betjeman imagines losing a very dear friend to a long and agonizing terminal disease. The first stanza is characterized by emotional distancing in which the focus is on the disease, which Betjeman further

distances by referring to it only as 'it'. The poem grows more
personal as he watches his friend become more remote as he
accepts the inevitable end, and then it concludes with a sense of
wonder as he receives his friend's final goodbye as a benediction.
In contrast is the poem 'Five o'Clock Shadow', in which
Betjeman imagines himself a patient in the terminal ward of a
hospital. The dominant impression is one of betrayal: the dying
patients feel betrayed both by their own bodies and by the
world of the living. While they endure physical and emotional
agonies, a group of doctors heads out for a round of golf,
nurses take their late-afternoon breaks and visiting family
members anticipate a comfortable evening at home. The poem's
title brilliantly captures the dual sense of the passing of one's
time and the lengthening of shadows to illustrate the terror
and isolation that only the dying can know. 'Old Friends' is an
elegiac lament for a colloquy of lost acquaintances, and conse-
quently this poem is infused with a much more intense and
personal sense of loss. Though Betjeman's spirits have sunk at
the memory of dead friends, his mood is lightened by an arrest-
ingly beautiful Cornish sunset, the coastal tidepools and the
distant chiming of the bells of St Minver's. The emergence of the
stars and the stillness of Daymer Bay remind him of the
wideness in God's mercy; however, he finds consolation not in
the Christian hope of eternity but in the dawning awareness that
he, the deceased, and the Celtic saints of the distant past are all
united in an eternity of stars and sea.

Two poems in this section stand apart in their level of intensity
and emotional forthrightness. Both examine Betjeman's reaction
to the deaths of his parents. Because his recollection of his dead
father starts with a painting, 'On the Portrait of a Deaf Man'
suggests that Betjeman is attempting to objectify his grief.
However, his repressed sorrow is supplanted by emotions and
images that are more painful yet: the images of a decaying
corpse, painful in themselves, are accompanied by the spiritual
pain of disbelief in the promise of a reunion in eternity.

'Remorse' is a poem no less painful, but the pain is of a very different sort. Betjeman recalls his mother's slow decline and death, contrasting her nurse's cold professionalism with his feelings of regret at having been neglectful of her. Finding little consolation in his faith, or in the theological disputes that had occupied him at this time, Betjeman says that creed and dogma pale in importance with how we show our love. The deepest contrast between these two poems is found not in his state of belief or unbelief at the points of his parents' deaths but in what his reactions to their deaths reveal about the filial bond with each. Betjeman's inability to consider his father now in any condition but decay is merely a continuation of the antipathy and tension that characterized their relationship when his father was living. His desperate wish to hear his mother's laboured breathing one more time suggests a subconscious need to carry an unnecessary burden of remorse. In neither poem is a mature relationship with his parents revealed, and in neither poem has death brought a full sense of closure.

Such closure is manifest in 'The Last Laugh', the final poem in Betjeman's final collection of poems, *A Nip in the Air*.[1] 'The Last Laugh' is also one of his shortest, its brevity symbolizing the sudden onset of death. In this poem Betjeman feels he has come to terms with his life and at last seems at peace with how he has lived it. Now he has one more request to make of life before he departs it. 'Give me the bonus of laughter' is his plea for equanimity and joy in the face of death, for release from the burden of anxiety in the last days of his life. The title suggests then that the last laugh will be Betjeman's and not death's. We might read this poem as his triumph over his fear of dying.

---

[1]   John Betjeman, *A Nip in the Air* (London: John Murray, 1974).

For Nineteenth-Century Burials

This cold weather
Carries so many old people away.
Quavering voices and blankets and breath
Go silent together.
The gentle fingers are touching to pray
Which crumple and straighten for Death.
These cold breezes
Carry the bells away on the air,
Stuttering tales of Gothic, and pass,
Catching new grave flowers into their hair,
Beating the chapel and red-coloured glass.

Devonshire Street W.1[1]

The heavy mahogany door with its wrought-iron screen
Shuts. And the sound is rich, sympathetic, discreet.
The sun still shines on this eighteenth-century scene
With Edwardian faience adornments—Devonshire Street.

No hope. And the X-ray photographs under his arm
Confirm the message. His wife stands timidly by.
The opposite brick-built house looks lofty and calm
Its chimneys steady against a mackerel sky.

No hope. And the iron nob of this palisade
So cold to the touch, is luckier now than he
'Oh merciless, hurrying Londoners! Why was I made
For the long and the painful deathbed coming to me?'

She puts her fingers in his as, loving and silly,
At long-past Kensington dances she used to do
'It's cheaper to take the tube to Piccadilly
And then we can catch a nineteen or a twenty-two.'

---

[1] The setting of King Edward VII's Hospital in Regents Park, London.

Death in Leamington

She died in the upstairs bedroom
　　By the light of the ev'ning star
That shone through the plate glass window
　　From over Leamington Spa.

Beside her the lonely crochet
　　Lay patiently and unstirred,
But the fingers that would have work'd it
　　Were dead as the spoken word.

And Nurse came in with the tea-things
　　Breast high 'mid the stands and chairs—
But Nurse was alone with her own little soul,
　　And the things were alone with theirs.

She bolted the big round window,
　　She let the blinds unroll,
She set a match to the mantle,
　　She covered the fire with coal.

And 'Tea!' she said in a tiny voice
　　'Wake up! It's nearly *five*.'
Oh! Chintzy, chintzy cheeriness,
　　Half dead and half alive!

Do you know that the stucco is peeling?
　　Do you know that the heart will stop?
From those yellow Italianate arches
　　Do you hear the plaster drop?

Nurse looked at the silent bedstead,
    At the gray, decaying face,
As the calm of a Leamington ev'ning
    Drifted into the place.

She moved the table of bottles
    Away from the bed to the wall;
And tiptoeing gently over the stairs
    Turned down the gas in the hall.

The Cottage Hospital

At the end of a long-walled garden
    in a red provincial town,
A brick path led to a mulberry—
    scanty grass at its feet.
I lay under blackening branches
    where the mulberry leaves hung down
Sheltering ruby fruit globes
    from a Sunday-tea-time heat.
Apple and plum espaliers
    basked upon bricks of brown;
The air was swimming with insects,
    and children played in the street.

Out of this bright intentness
    into the mulberry shade
Musca domestica (housefly)
    swung from the August light
Slap into slithery rigging
    by the waiting spider made
Which spun the lithe elastic
    till the fly was shrouded tight.
Down came the hairy talons
    and horrible poison blade
And none of the garden noticed
    that fizzing, hopeless fight.

Say in what Cottage Hospital
   whose pale green walls resound
With the tap upon polished parquet
   of inflexible nurses' feet
Shall I myself be lying
   when they range the screens around?
And say shall I groan in dying,
   as I twist the sweaty sheet?
Or gasp for breath uncrying,
   as I feel my senses drown'd
While the air is swimming with insects
   and children play in the street?

House of Rest

Now all the world she knew is dead
    In this small room she lives her days
The wash-hand stand and single bed
    Screened from the public gaze.

The horse-brass shines, the kettle sings,
    The cup of China tea
Is tasted among cared-for things
    Ranged round for me to see—

Lincoln, by Valentine and Co.,[1]
    Now yellowish brown and stained,
But there some fifty years ago
    Her Harry was ordained;

Outside the Church at Woodhall Spa
    The smiling groom and bride,
And here's his old tobacco jar
    Dried lavender inside.

I do not like to ask if he
    Was 'High' or 'Low' or 'Broad'
Lest such a question seem to be
    A mockery of Our Lord.

Her full grey eyes look far beyond
    The little room and me
To village church and village pond
    And ample rectory.

---

[1] An early photographic company, based in Dundee, they began to produce topographic
prints in the 1860s that proved extremely popular with middle-class families.

She sees her children each in place
    Eyes downcast as they wait,
She hears her Harry murmur Grace,
    Then heaps the porridge plate.

Aroused at seven, to bed by ten,
    They fully lived each day,
Dead sons, so motor-bike mad then,
    And daughters far away.

Now when the bells for Eucharist
    Sound in the Market Square,
With sunshine struggling through the mist
    And Sunday in the air,

The veil between her and her dead
    Dissolves and shows them clear,
The Consecration Prayer is said
    And all of them are near.

Variation on a Theme by
T. W. Rolleston[1]

Under the ground, on a Saturday afternoon in winter
    Lies a mother of five,
And frost has bitten the purple November rose flowers
    Which budded when *she* was alive.

They have switched on the street lamps here by the
    cemet'ry railing;
    In the dying afternoon
Men from football, and women from Timothy White's
    and McIlroy's
    Will be coming teawards soon.

But her place is empty in the queue at the International,
    The greengrocer's queue lacks one,
So does the crowd at MacFisheries. There's no one to
    go to Freeman's
    To ask if the shoes are done.

Will she, who was so particular, be glad to know that
    after
    The tears, the prayers and the priest,
Her clothing coupons and ration book were handed in
    at the Food Office
    For the files marked 'deceased'?

---

[1] T.W. Rolleston (1857–1920) was an Irish poet most famous for 'The Dead at Clonmacnois.'

Variation on a Theme by Newbolt[1]

The City will see him no more at important meetings
  In Renaissance board rooms by Edwin Cooper designed;
In his numerous clubs the politely jocular greetings
  Will be rather more solemn today with his death in mind.

Half mast from a first floor window, the Company's bunting
  Flops over Leadenhall Street in this wintry air
And his fellow directors, baulked of a good day's hunting
  Nod gloomily back to the gloomy commissionaire.

His death will be felt through the whole of the organization,
  In every branch of its vast managerial tree,
His brother-in-law we suppose will attend the cremation,
  A service will later be held in St Katherine Cree.

But what of his guns?—he was always a generous giver.
  (Oh yes, of course, we will each of us send a wreath),
His yacht? and his shoot? and his beautiful reach of river?
  And all the clubs in his locker at Walton Heath?

I do not know, for my mind sees one thing only,
  A luxurious bedroom looking on miles of fir
From a Surrey height where his widow sits silent and lonely
  For the man whose love seemed wholly given to her.

---

[1] Sir Henry Newbolt (1862–1938) was an English poet and historian known for his poetry about the sea.

I.M.
Walter Ramsden[1]
ob. March 26, 1947
Pembroke College, Oxford

Dr. Ramsden cannot read *The Times* obituary today
    He's dead.
Let monographs on silk worms by other people be
    Thrown away
    Unread
For he who best could understand and criticize them, he
    Lies clay
    In bed.

The body waits in Pembroke College where the ivy taps
      the panes
    All night;
That old head so full of knowledge, that good heart that
      kept the brains
    All right,
Those old cheeks that faintly flushed as the port suffused
      the veins,
Drain'd white.

Crocus in the Fellows' Garden, winter jasmine up the wall
    Gleam gold.
Shadows of Victorian chimneys on the sunny grassplot
      fall
    Long, cold.
Master, Bursar, Senior Tutor, these, his three survivors, all
    Feel old.

---

[1] Professor of Biochemistry and Fellow of Pembroke College, Oxford.

They remember, as the coffin to its final obsequations
    Leaves the gates,
Buzz of bees in window boxes on their summer
       ministrations,
    Kitchen din,
    Cups and plates,
And the getting of bump suppers for the long-dead
       generations
    Coming in,
    From Eights.

Inevitable

First there was putting hot-water bottles to it,
   Then there was seeing what an osteopath could do,
Then trying drugs to coax the thing and woo it,
   Then came the time when he knew that he was through.

Now in his hospital bed I see him lying
   Limp on the pillows like a cast-off Teddy bear.
Is he too ill to know that he is dying?
   And, if he does know, does he really care?

Grey looks the ward with November's overcasting
   But his large eyes seem to see beyond the day;
Speech becomes sacred near silence everlasting
   Oh if I *must* speak, have I words to say?

In the past weeks we had talked about Variety,
   Vesta Victoria, Lew Lake and Wilkie Bard,[1]
Horse-buses, hansoms, crimes in High Society—
   Although we knew his death was near, we fought against it
     hard.

Now from his remoteness in a stillness unaccountable
   He drags himself to earth again to say good-bye to me—
His final generosity when almost insurmountable
   The barriers and mountains he has crossed again must be.

---

[1]   Bard (1874–1944) and Victoria (1873–1951) were popular performers in the music
halls. Lake (1874-1939) was a film actor.

Five o'Clock Shadow

This is the time of day when we in the Men's Ward
   Think 'One more surge of the pain and I give up the fight,'
When he who struggles for breath can struggle less strongly:
   This is the time of day which is worse than night.

A haze of thunder hangs on the hospital rose-beds,
   A doctors' foursome out on the links is played,
Safe in her sitting-room Sister is putting her feet up:
   This is the time of day when we feel betrayed.

Below the windows, loads of loving relations
   Rev in the car park, changing gear at the bend,
Making for home and a nice big tea and the telly:
   'Well, we've done what we can. It can't be long till the end.'

This is the time of day when the weight of bedclothes
   Is harder to bear than a sharp incision of steel.
The endless anonymous croak of a cheap transistor
   Intensifies the lonely terror I feel.

Old Friends

The sky widens to Cornwall. A sense of sea
    Hangs in the lichenous branches and still there's light.
The road from its tunnel of blackthorn rises free
    To a final height,

And over the west is glowing a mackerel sky
    Whose opal fleece has faded to purple pink.
In this hour of the late-lit, listening evening, why
    Do my spirits sink?

The tide is high and a sleepy Atlantic sends
    Exploring ripple on ripple down Polzeath shore,
And the gathering dark is full of the thought of friends
    I shall see no more.

Where is Anne Channel who loved this place the best,
    With her tense blue eyes and her shopping-bag falling
        apart,
And her racy gossip and nineteen-twenty zest,
    And warmth of heart?

Where's Roland, easing his most unwieldy car,
    With its load of golf-clubs, backwards into the lane?
Where's Kathleen Stokes with her Sealyhams? There's
        Doom Bar;
        Bray Hill shows plain;

For this is the turn, and the well-known trees draw near;
    On the road their pattern in moonlight fades and
        swells:
As the engine stops, from two miles off I hear
    St Minver bells.

What a host of stars in a wideness still and deep:
    What a host of souls, as a motor-bike whines away
And the silver snake of the estuary curls to sleep
    In Daymer Bay.

Are they one with the Celtic saints and the years between?
    Can they see the moonlit pools where ribbonweed
        drifts?
As I reach our hill, I am part of a sea unseen—
    And oppression lifts.

On a Portrait of a Deaf Man

The kind old face, the egg-shaped head,
  The tie, discreetly loud,
The loosely fitting shooting clothes,
  A closely fitting shroud.

He liked old City dining-rooms,
  Potatoes in their skin,
But now his mouth is wide to let
  The London clay come in.

He took me on long silent walks
  In country lanes when young,
He knew the name of ev'ry bird
  But not the song it sung.

And when he could not hear me speak
  He smiled and looked so wise
That now I do not like to think
  Of maggots in his eyes.

He liked the rain-washed Cornish air
  And smell of ploughed-up soil,
He liked a landscape big and bare
  And painted it in oil.

But least of all he liked that place
  Which hangs on Highgate Hill
Of soaked Carrara-covered earth
  For Londoners to fill.

He would have liked to say good-bye,
    Shake hands with many friends,
In Highgate now his finger-bones
    Stick through his finger-ends.

You, God, who treat him thus and thus,
    Say 'Save his soul and pray.'
You ask me to believe You and
    I only see decay.

Remorse

The lungs draw in the air and rattle it out again;
  The eyes revolve in their sockets and upwards stare;
No more worry and waiting and troublesome doubt again—
  She whom I loved and left is no longer there.

The nurse puts down her knitting and walks across to her,
  With quick professional eye she surveys the dead.
Just one patient the less and little the loss to her,
  Distantly tender she settles the shrunken head.

Protestant claims and Catholic, the wrong and the right of
    them,
  Unimportant they seem in the face of death—
But my neglect and unkindness—to lose the sight of them
  I would listen even again to that labouring breath.

The Last Laugh

I made hay while the sun shone.
    My work sold.
Now, if the harvest is over
    And the world cold,
Give me the bonus of laughter
    As I lose hold.

3

Belief

3 Belief

Although John Betjeman was greatly preoccupied by a fear of death and by uncertainties about his eternal destiny, and indeed about the existence of God, these anxieties were held in a kind of creative tension with his belief and resolve in his Christian faith. The poems in this chapter reveal how at times he found faith in the encouraging example of others, or by way of an occasional spontaneous overflow of spiritual emotion, or even in the paradox of a rational acceptance of divine mystery. In describing his belief, Betjeman's tone in these poems ranges from intellectual objectivity, to monastic devotion, to emotional jubilance and even to jocular levity. His faith was too complex and multifaceted to manifest itself in only one fashion. Belief was no simple matter for him, even when he felt a measure of security in his faith, and these poems reveal that he brought intellectual honesty and spiritual depth to his poetic reflections on Christian belief.

The first four poems are united by a common theme: the constructive influence on Betjeman's faith of the spiritual journeys of others. 'The Commander' reveals the communal faith to be a fundamental element in Betjeman's life, one the poet equates with other virtues he treasured so highly: the bonds of family and friendship, a delight in English architecture, a respect for nature, and the importance of human decency. In this tribute to George Barnes, a senior BBC official who died in 1960, Betjeman honours his friend by attributing to his example the necessity of accepting the onset of death with humility and embracing a simple trust in God's promise of eternal life.

'Felixstowe' begins with mournful seaside echoes of Matthew Arnold's 'Dover Beach'; however in contrast to Arnold's exploration of the loss of faith, Betjeman's speaker – a nun who is the last surviving member of her order – continues to find faith in God's love, despite her isolation and loneliness. She observes the world going about its daily business, oblivious to her and to the work of God, and in spite of worldly temptation her devotion and faith never waver.

Both 'Saint Cadoc' and 'The Conversion of St Paul', though very different sorts of poems, show the examples of saints' lives increasing the poet's faith. 'Saint Cadoc', a tribute to the Celtic mysticism of a sixth-century Cornish saint, evokes an intense pitch of emotional religiosity. As he treads the ocean paths once walked by Cadoc, Betjeman petitions the saint to pray for him and begins to celebrate the natural unity of all things in God – sea, earth, saint and poet. In the end, he finds his solace from the fear of death in the comforts of Celtic Christianity. In contrast, 'The Conversion of St Paul' exemplifies Greek rationalism and stoicism as Betjeman ponders the faith of the Church's founding apostle. The poem's occasion – a public response to an agnostic's attacks on Christianity on BBC radio – demands that the troubling questions of faith be dealt with in a logical and rational manner. Betjeman thus argues in verse that St Paul's conversion, though more dramatic than the typical Christian's, serves yet to model conversion for all believers. Paul's initial rejection of Christianity is what made him so committed and effective an apostle and so devout in his faith. Betjeman also uses the story of Paul's conversion to describe his own. As a tolerant Anglican, he knows that no conversion experience can provide a formula for all believers: some see Jesus and never lose his presence, while others see once and never see again. But most believers, Betjeman argues, constantly experience Christ's 'fitful glow', a symbol of the ebb and flow of faith in the heart of the struggling believer.

Elements of Celtic Christianity, particularly the idea of the immanence of God in the natural world, can be seen in the next three poems, 'Uffington', 'Wantage Bells' and 'Autumn 1964'. These poems are characterized by a spontaneous and joyful outburst at the discovery of God not in a church but in nature, a discovery made more profound by the unexpected ringing of church bells. 'Uffington' begins with an ambiguous image describing the tension of village church bells: Betjeman's marvellous use of consonance in 'peal' and 'pall' symbolizes the crux of the poem, the fearful and majestic power of divine mystery. The church bells seem to summon the very presence of God, yet they also remind us of impending death. This duality captures Betjeman's uncertainty about the nature of the divine and the necessity of accepting some ambiguity as inevitable in a life of faith. In 'Wantage Bells' he encounters God quite plainly in a garden. Although it is a spring Sunday morning and church bells are sounding, it is the prolific and arresting beauty of his garden, not the bells, that arouses Betjeman. The bells subconsciously remind him that this garden is not an accident of nature but is in fact the intentional and most generous gift of a Creator who remains present in his creation. It was not church where the poet found God, although church did subtly remind him of God's bounty and love. In fact, Betjeman may be suggesting here that God is as likely to be found in nature as in church. 'Autumn 1964' emphasizes a balanced and reciprocal relationship between God's creation and man's institutional efforts to celebrate and preserve for eternity the fact of the Incarnation. During a glowing autumn Sunday sunrise, the poet anticipates the approaching bells of worship, which will peal out in praise not of God himself but of the beauty of God's creation as evidence of his immanence. In response, all of creation joins in praising God's gift of eternal life, which Betjeman depicts in the language of baptism and salvation. The astonishing beauty of creation is material evidence of God's reckless generosity. No element of Christian worship can adequately honour or thank God for his bounty, let alone reciprocate; all Christian worship can do is to remind us of the utter profundity of his gift.

Betjeman senses that we always live in the presence of divine mystery; he cannot explain it, but he does not doubt that his feeling is based in genuine truth.

The mystery of Christian faith is a central issue in the next four poems: 'Churchyards', 'Lenten Thoughts of a High Anglican', 'Advent 1955' and 'Christmas'. In these poems, the sudden and wondrous appearance of God in the most unlikely of places gives Betjeman a sense of spiritual security and renders him susceptible to the embrace of mystery and miracle. These poems are also characterized by an unusual tonal complexity that weds the high seriousness and rationalism of 'The Conversion of St Paul' with a joviality that typifies much of Betjeman's light verse. 'Churchyards' is an especially deceptive poem in its use of light-hearted rhythms to convey a seriousness about death and faith. The poem amuses first by recounting the churchyard's shared history with the alehouse, using this fact to remind us that churches preserve the history of communities and, by extension, of the nation as well. Yet it is in the traditional churchyard that Betjeman says we are likely to encounter God, because in these ancient burying grounds are village faithful who believed that after death they would receive new bodies and the gift of eternal life. Despite the poem's jaunty tone, however, Betjeman's lines ring out with a sense of disappointment in his and his culture's inability to believe with such complete security as generations past. In 'Lenten Thoughts of a High Anglican', Betjeman describes a mysterious and sexually alluring woman who receives Communion each Sunday. In an effort to increase his parishioners' attentiveness, the minister has told his congregation not to stare around and become distracted during the church service. But Betjeman's experience contradicts the minister's warning: perversely, God comes to him via the mysterious and alluring woman. What better illustration could one find of the principle that God's manifestations are surprising and extraordinary than in these two poems? Whether fantasizing about a woman's sexual life or contemplating the history of English village life, Betjeman suddenly becomes aware of the presence of God. The intrigue and arousal surrounding the 'mistress' speaks to Betjeman of God's mysteriousness; while the churchyard, with its history of simple belief and communal life, teaches him simply to embrace the mystery of faith.

With similar wonder and humour, 'Advent 1955' and 'Christmas' both satirize the materialism inherent in the secular celebrations of that festival. The simplicity of Christ's nativity in a humble barn becomes a revelation for Betjeman, particularly when contrasted with the vanity and folly of decorations, ludicrous gifts and obsessions with Christmas cards. In both poems, Betjeman reminds us that Advent is the season for us to prepare for the gift of God to humanity, without which we would, quite simply, not be able to live in the presence of the divine. 'Christmas' in particular reminds us of the contrast between the triviality of our holiday festivity and the majesty and mystery of Christmas's true import: the Incarnation. Betjeman juxtaposes the banality of our celebrations of Christmas against the metaphysical reality of God becoming man, of the divine presenting itself to us. In the midst of mundanity comes the astonishing appearance of God. For Betjeman, the mystery is so profound, so inexplicable, that all human efforts to celebrate this signal event of Christianity fail to offer appropriate glory. The gifts we exchange with each other – our symbolic re-enactment of God's gift – are no less trivial and base than our effort at honouring God in worship. In the midst of normal human triviality appeared God incarnate, and yet more mysterious, the poem concludes, is the fact that God remains incarnate today in the metaphysical reality of the Eucharist.

Faith in the Eucharist to embody the real presence of Christ is at the heart of the final two poems of this group: 'In Willesden Churchyard' and 'A Lincolnshire Church'. 'In Willesden Churchyard' is an elegiac meditation on the encroaching of blight on pastoralism and of doubt on faith. Betjeman's speculation about the lives of those buried here points to his recurring anxiety about death and eternity. Symbolizing the loss of England's pastoral past in tombstones pitted by chemical pollution, he succumbs to fears of his own flesh decaying. But in the midst of this reverie he moves from a fear of death in the absence of God to an awareness of God's 'immanence' in the church nearby. Although the word 'glows' suggests God's vital intensity, Betjeman's spatial separation from God seems to deny him full communion; God is in the church while the poet remains in the churchyard. Perhaps the sacrament ameliorates his fear, but perhaps Betjeman remains fearful of death despite the proximity of the sacrament: that God is present in the church but absent for him. The ambiguity of belief is the very means to a stronger faith, as 'A Lincolnshire Church' shows, a church that interests him not for its architecture or its faith but for its embodiment of the communal spirit of Lincolnshire's wolds and marshes and the larger spirit of 'Dear old, bloody old England'. As soon as Betjeman enters the church, however, he senses something more profound: the mysterious presence of the divine. Despite his attempts to separate himself socially and spiritually from other English sinners, he begins to realize that all believers are united in a spiritual community that transcends the walls of social distinction that our innate snobbery urges us to build. As the church door shuts behind him, he falls to his knees, aware that God is both spirit and flesh; being in the presence of this mystery excites him spiritually, though he cannot explain or define it. After confessing his sinfulness, he becomes aware of a priest in the church, an Indian whose presence in a Lincolnshire village parish church he finds inexplicable. Sharing the presence of the divine with this priest creates a spiritual union more vital and profound than any social union. Here at the altar, where this meeting occurs, is where God becomes incarnate in the Eucharist. This is 'where the white light flickers', where the poet can see only darkly, where truth cannot be determined absolutely, where the known and unknown come face to face. This, Betjeman tells us, is where we approach God – or he approaches us.

The Commander[1]

On a shining day of October we remembered you, Commander,
  When the trees were gold and still
And some of their boughs were green where the whip of the
    wind had missed them
  On this nippy Staffordshire hill.

A clean sky streamed through institutional windows
  As we heard the whirr of Time
Touching our Quaker silence, in builders' lorries departing
  For Newcastle-under-Lyme.

The proving words of the psalm you bequeathed to the gowned
    assembly
  On waiting silence broke,
'Lord, I am not high-minded . . .' In the youthful voice of
    the student
  Your own humility spoke.

I remembered our shared delight in architecture and nature
  As bicycling we went
By saffron-spotted palings to crumbling box-pewed churches
  Down hazel lanes in Kent.

I remembered on winter evenings, with wine and the family
    round you,
  Your reading Dickens aloud
And the laughs we used to have at your gift for administration,
  For you were never proud.

---

[1] Sir George Reginald Barnes (1904–60) spent much of his career in the BBC and was
  its first director of television. He was a great friend of Betjeman.

Sky and sun and the sea! the greatness of things was in you
   And thus you refrained your soul.
Let others fuss over academical detail,
   You saw people whole.

'Lord, I am not high-minded . . .' The final lesson you taught me,
   When you bade the world good-bye,
Was humbly and calmly to trust in the soul's survival
   When my own hour comes to die.

Felixstowe, *or*
The Last of Her Order

With one consuming roar along the shingle
      The long wave claws and rakes the pebbles down
To where its backwash and the next wave mingle,
      A mounting arch of water weedy-brown
Against the tide the off-shore breezes blow.
Oh wind and water, this is Felixstowe.

In winter when the sea winds chill and shriller
      Than those of summer, all their cold unload
Full on the gimcrack attic of the villa
      Where I am lodging off the Orwell Road,
I put my final shilling in the meter
And only make my loneliness completer.

In eighteen ninety-four when we were founded,
      Counting our Reverend Mother we were six,
How full of hope we were and prayer-surrounded
      'The Little Sisters of the Hanging Pyx'.[1]
We built our orphanage. We ran our school.
Now only I am left to keep the rule.

Here in the gardens of the Spa Pavilion
      Warm in the whisper of a summer sea,
The cushioned scabious, a deep vermilion,
      With white pins stuck in it, looks up at me
A sun-lit kingdom touched by butterflies
And so my memory of winter dies.

---

[1] A pyx is a vessel in which consecrated bread is reserved. Betjeman is being very whimsical here.

Across the grass the poplar shades grow longer
    And louder clang the waves along the coast.
The band packs up. The evening breeze is stronger
    And all the world goes home to tea and toast.
I hurry past a cakeshop's tempting scones
Bound for the red brick twilight of St John's.

'Thou knowest my down sitting and mine uprising'
    Here where the white light burns with steady glow
Safe from the vain world's silly sympathizing,
    Safe with the Love that I was born to know,
Safe from the surging of the lonely sea
My heart finds rest, my heart finds rest in Thee.

Saint Cadoc[1]

A flame of rushlight in the cell
On holy walls and holy well
And to the west the thundering bay
With soaking seaweed, sand and spray,
    Oh good St Cadoc pray for me
    Here in your cell beside the sea.

Somewhere the tree, the yellowing oak,
Is waiting for the woodman's stroke,
Waits for the chisel saw and plane
To prime it for the earth again
    And in the earth, for me inside,
    The generous oak tree will have died.

St Cadoc blest the woods of ash
Bent landwards by the Western lash,
He loved the veinéd threshold stones
Where sun might sometimes bleach his bones
    He had no cowering fear of death
    For breath of God was Cadoc's breath.

Some cavern generates the germs
To send my body to the worms,
Today some red hands make the shell
To blow my soul away to Hell
    Today a pair walks newly married
    Along the path where I'll be carried.

---

[1]   A sixth-century Welsh priest martyred by Saxons while serving Mass, Cadoc is the
patron saint of scrofula, deafness, cramps and glandular disorders.

St Cadoc, when the wind was high,
Saw angels in the Cornish sky
As ocean rollers curled and poured
Their loud Hosannas to the Lord,
    His little cell was not too small
    For that great Lord who made them all.

Here where St Cadoc sheltered God
The archaeologist has trod,
Yet death is now the gentle shore
With Land upon the cliffs before
    And in his cell beside the sea
    The Celtic saint has prayed for me.

The Conversion of St Paul

Now is the time when we recall
The sharp Conversion of St Paul.
Converted! Turned the wrong way round—
A man who seemed till then quite sound,
Keen on religion—very keen—
No one, it seems, had ever been
So keen on persecuting those
Who said that Christ was God and chose
To die for this absurd belief
As Christ had died beside the thief.
Then in a sudden blinding light
Paul knew that Christ was God all right—
And very promptly lost his sight.
Poor Paul! They led him by the hand
He who had been so high and grand
A helpless blunderer, fasting, waiting,
Three days inside himself debating
In physical blindness: 'As it's true
That Christ is God and died for you,
Remember all the things you did
To keep His gospel message hid.
Remember how you helped them even
To throw the stones that murdered Stephen.
And do you think that you are strong
Enough to own that you were wrong?'
They must have been an awful time,
Those three long days repenting crime
Till Ananias came and Paul
Received his sight, and more than all
His former strength, and was baptised.
Saint Paul is often criticised

By modern people who're annoyed
At his conversion, saying Freud
Explains it all. But they omit
The really vital point of it,
Which isn't *how* it was achieved
But what it was that Paul believed.
He knew as certainly as we
Know you are you and I am me
That Christ was all He claimed to be.
What is conversion? Turning round
From chaos to a love profound.
And chaos too is an abyss
In which the only life is this.
Such a belief is quite all right
If you are sure like Mrs. Knight[1]
And think morality will do
For all the ills we're subject to.
But raise your eyes and see with Paul
An explanation of it all.
Injustice, cancer's cruel pain,
All suffering that seems in vain,
The vastness of the universe,
Creatures like centipedes and worse—
All part of an enormous plan
Which mortal eyes can never scan
And out of it came God to man.
Jesus is God and came to show
The world we live in here below
Is just an antechamber where
We for His Father's house prepare.
What is conversion? Not at all
For me the experience of St Paul,
No blinding light, a fitful glow

---

[1] Margaret Knight had attacked Christianity on BBC radio in 1955.

Is all the light of faith I know
Which sometimes goes completely out
And leaves me plunging round in doubt
Until I will myself to go
And worship in God's house below—
My parish Church—and even there
I find distractions everywhere.

What is Conversion? Turning round
To gaze upon a love profound.
For some of us see Jesus plain
And never once look back again,
And some of us have seen and known
And turned and gone away alone,
But most of us turn slow to see
The figure hanging on a tree
And stumble on and blindly grope
Upheld by intermittent hope.
God grant before we die we all
May see the light as did St Paul.

Uffington

Tonight we feel the muffled peal
   Hang on the village like a pall;
It overwhelms the towering elms—
   That death-reminding dying fall;
The very sky no longer high
   Comes down within the reach of all.
Imprisoned in a cage of sound
Even the trivial seems profound.

Wantage Bells

Now with the bells through the apple bloom
    Sunday-ly sounding
And the prayers of the nuns in their chapel gloom
    Us all surrounding,
Where the brook flows
Brick walls of rose
Send on the motionless meadow the bell notes
        rebounding.

Wall flowers are bright in their beds
    And their scent all pervading,
Withered are primroses' heads
    And the hyacinth fading
But flowers by the score
Multitudes more
Weed flowers and seed flowers and mead flowers our
        paths are invading.

Where are the words to express
    Such a reckless bestowing?
The voices of birds utter less
    Than the thanks we are owing,
Bell notes alone
Ring praise of their own
As clear as the weed-waving brook and as evenly flowing.

Autumn 1964

Red apples hang like globes of light
   Against this pale November haze,
And now, although the mist is white,
   In half-an-hour a day of days
Will climb into its golden height
   And Sunday bells will ring its praise.

The sparkling flint, the darkling yew,
   The red brick, less intensely red
Than hawthorn berries bright with dew
   Or leaves of creeper still unshed,
The watery sky washed clean and new,
   Are all rejoicing with the dead.

The yellowing elm shows yet some green,
   The mellowing bells exultant sound:
Never have light and colour been
   So prodigally thrown around;
And in the bells the promise tells
   Of greater light where Love is found.

Churchyards

Now when the weather starts to clear
How fresh the primrose clumps appear,
Those shining pools of springtime flower
In our churchyard. And on the tower
We see the sharp spring sunlight thrown
On all its sparkling rainwashed stone,
That tower, so built to take the light
Of sun by day and moon by night,
That centuries of weather there
Have mellowed it to twice as fair
As when it first rose new and hard
Above the sports in our churchyard.

    For churchyards then, though hallowed ground,
Were not so grim as now they sound,
And horns of ale were handed round
For which churchwardens used to pay
On each especial vestry day.
'Twas thus the village drunk its beer
With its relations buried near,
And that is why we often see
Inns where the alehouse used to be
Close to the church when prayers were said
And Masses for the village dead.

    But in these latter days we've grown
To think that the memorial stone
Is quite enough for soul and clay
Until the Resurrection day.
Perhaps it is. It's not for me
To argue on theology.

    But this I know, you're sure to find
Some headstones of the Georgian kind

In each old churchyard near and far,
Just go and see how fine they are.
Notice the lettering of that age
Spaced like a noble title-page,
The parish names cut deep and strong
To hold the shades of evening long,
The quaint and sometimes touching rhymes
By parish poets of the times,
Bellows, or reaping hook or spade
To show, perhaps, the dead man's trade,
And cherubs in the corner spaces
With wings and English ploughboy faces.

Engraved on slate or carved in stone
These Georgian headstones hold their own
With craftsmanship of earlier days
Men gave in their Creator's praise.
More homely are they than the white
Italian marbles which were quite
The rage in Good Kind Edward's reign,
With ugly lettering, hard and plain.

Our churches are our history shown
In wood and glass and iron and stone.
I hate to see in old churchyards
Tombstones stacked round like playing cards
Along the wall which then encloses
A trim new lawn and standard roses,
Bird-baths and objects such as fill a
Garden in some suburban villa.
The Bishop comes; the bird-bath's blessed,
Our churchyard's now 'a garden of rest'.
And so it may be, all the same
Graveyard's a much more honest name.

Oh why do people waste their breath
Inventing dainty names for death?
On the old tombstones of the past

We do not read 'At peace at last'
But simply 'died' or plain 'departed'.
It's no good being chicken-hearted.
We die; that's that; our flesh decays
Or disappears in other ways.
But since we're Christians, we believe
That we new bodies will receive
To clothe our souls for us to meet
Our Maker at his Judgement Seat.
And this belief's a gift of faith
And, if it's true, no end is death.
  Mid-Lent is passed and Easter's near
The greatest day of all the year
When Jesus, who indeed had died,
Rose with his body glorified.
And if you find believing hard
The primroses in your churchyard
And modern science too will show
That all things change the while they grow,
And we, who change in Time will be
Still more changed in Eternity.

Lenten Thoughts of a High Anglican

Isn't she lovely, 'the Mistress'?
    With her wide-apart grey-green eyes,
The droop of her lips and, when she smiles,
    Her glance of amused surprise?

How nonchalantly she wears her clothes,
    How expensive they are as well!
And the sound of her voice is as soft and deep
    As the Christ Church tenor bell.

But why do I call her 'the Mistress'
    Who know not her way of life?
Because she has more of a cared-for air
    Than many a legal wife.

How elegantly she swings along
    In the vapoury incense veil;
The angel choir must pause in song
    When she kneels at the altar rail.

The parson said that we shouldn't stare
    Around when we come to church,
Or the Unknown God we are seeking
    May forever elude our search.

But I hope the preacher will not think
    It unorthodox and odd
If I add that I glimpse in 'the Mistress'
    A hint of the Unknown God.

Advent 1955

The Advent wind begins to stir
With sea-like sounds in our Scotch fir,
It's dark at breakfast, dark at tea,
And in between we only see
Clouds hurrying across the sky
And rain-wet roads the wind blows dry
And branches bending to the gale
Against great skies all silver-pale.
The world seems travelling into space,
And travelling at a faster pace
Than in the leisured summer weather
When we and it sit out together,
For now we feel the world spin round
On some momentous journey bound—
Journey to what? to whom? to where?
The Advent bells call out 'Prepare,
Your world is journeying to the birth
Of God made Man for us on earth.'
    And how, in fact, do we prepare
For the great day that waits us there—
The twenty-fifth day of December,
The birth of Christ? For some it means
An interchange of hunting scenes
On coloured cards. And I remember
Last year I sent out twenty yards,
Laid end to end, of Christmas cards
To people that I scarcely know—
They'd sent a card to me, and so
I had to send one back. Oh dear!
Is this a form of Christmas cheer?
Or is it, which is less surprising,

My pride gone in for advertising?
The only cards that really count
Are that extremely small amount
From real friends who keep in touch
And are not rich but love us much.
Some ways indeed are very odd
By which we hail the birth of God.
We raise the price of things in shops,
We give plain boxes fancy tops
And lines which traders cannot sell
Thus parcell'd go extremely well.
We dole out bribes we call a present
To those to whom we must be pleasant
For business reasons. Our defence is
These bribes are charged against expenses
And bring relief in Income Tax.
Enough of these unworthy cracks!
'The time draws near the birth of Christ',
A present that cannot be priced
Given two thousand years ago.
Yet if God had not given so
He still would be a distant stranger
And not the Baby in the manger.

Christmas

The bells of waiting Advent ring,
    The Tortoise stove is lit again
And lamp-oil light across the night
    Has caught the streaks of winter rain
In many a stained-glass window sheen
From Crimson Lake to Hooker's Green.[1]

The holly in the windy hedge
    And round the Manor House the yew
Will soon be stripped to deck the ledge,
    The altar, font and arch and pew,
So that the villagers can say
'The church looks nice' on Christmas Day.

Provincial public houses blaze
    And Corporation tramcars clang,
On lighted tenements I gaze
    Where paper decorations hang,
And bunting in the red Town Hall
Says 'Merry Christmas to you all.'

And London shops on Christmas Eve
    Are strung with silver bells and flowers
As hurrying clerks the City leave
    To pigeon-haunted classic towers,
And marbled clouds go scudding by
The many-steepled London sky.

---

[1] Betjeman's wordplay has names of artists' colours functioning as imaginary places.

And girls in slacks remember Dad,
   And oafish louts remember Mum,
And sleepless children's hearts are glad,
   And Christmas-morning bells say 'Come!'
Even to shining ones who dwell
Safe in the Dorchester Hotel.

And is it true? And is it true,
   This most tremendous tale of all,
Seen in a stained-glass window's hue,
   A Baby in an ox's stall?
The Maker of the stars and sea
Become a Child on earth for me?

And is it true? For if it is,
   No loving fingers tying strings
Around those tissued fripperies,
   The sweet and silly Christmas things,
Bath salts and inexpensive scent
And hideous tie so kindly meant,

No love that in a family dwells
   No carolling in frosty air,
Nor all the steeple-shaking bells
   Can with this single Truth compare—
That God was Man in Palestine
And lives today in Bread and Wine.

In Willesden Churchyard[1]

Come walk with me, my love, to Neasden Lane.
The chemicals from various factories
Have bitten deep into the Portland stone
And streaked the white Carrara of the graves
Of many a Pooter[2] and his Caroline,
Long laid to rest among these dripping trees;
And that small heap of fast-decaying flowers
Marks Lupin Pooter lately gathered in;
And this, my love, is Laura Seymour's grave—
'So long the loyal counsellor and friend'
Of that Charles Reade[3] whose coffin lies with hers.
Was she his mistress? Did he visit her
When coming down from Oxford by the coach?
Alighting at the turnpike, did he walk
These elmy lanes of Middlesex and climb
A stile or two across the dairy farms
Over to Harlesden at the wicket gate?
Then the soft rigours of his Fellowship
Were tenderly relaxed. The sun would send
Last golden streaks of mild October light
On tarred and weather-boarded barn and shed.
Blue bonfire smoke would hang among the trees;
And in the little stucco hermitage
Did Laura gently stroke her lover's head?
And did her Charles look up into her eyes
For loyal counsel there? I do not know.

---

[1] The title refers to the parish church of St Mary in Neasden Lane.
[2] This is a reference to George and Weedon Grossmith's *Diary of a Nobody*. Charles Pooter is the diarist, Caroline his wife and Lupin his son.
[3] Charles Reade (1814–84) was an Oxford don, fellow of Magdalen College and author of *The Cloister and the Heart*. Laura Seymour, an actress, was Reade's mistress from 1853 until her death in 1879.

Doubtless some pedant for his Ph.D.
Has ascertained the facts, or I myself
Might find them in the public libraries.
I only know that as we see her grave
My flesh, to dissolution nearer now
Than yours, which is so milky white and soft,
Frightens me, though the Blessed Sacrament
Not ten yards off in Willesden parish church
Glows with the present immanence of God.

A Lincolnshire Church

Greyly tremendous the thunder
Hung over the width of the wold
But here the green marsh was alight
In a huge cloud cavern of gold,
And there, on a gentle eminence,
Topping some ash trees, a tower
Silver and brown in the sunlight,
Worn by sea-wind and shower,
Lincolnshire Middle Pointed.
And around it, turning their backs,
The usual sprinkle of villas;
The usual woman in slacks,
Cigarette in her mouth,
Regretting Americans, stands
As a wireless croons in the kitchen
Manicuring her hands.
Dear old, bloody old England
Of telegraph poles and tin,
Seemingly so indifferent
And with so little soul to win.
What sort of church, I wonder?[1]
The path is a grassy mat,
And grass is drowning the headstones
Sloping this way and that.
'Cathedral Glass' in the windows,
A roof of unsuitable slate—
Restored with a vengeance, for certain,
About eighteen-eighty-eight.

---

[1]   Bevis Hillier identifies this church as St Margaret's, Huttoft, near Sutton-on-Sea. See
John Betjeman: New Fame, New Love (London: John Murray, 2002), pp. 365 and
670.

The door swung easily open
(Unlocked, for these parts, is odd)
And there on the South aisle altar
Is the tabernacle of God.
There where the white light flickers
By the white and silver veil,
A wafer dipped in a wine-drop
Is the Presence the angels hail,
Is God who created the Heavens
And the wide green marsh as well
Who sings in the sky with the skylark
Who calls in the evening bell,
Is God who prepared His coming
With fruit of the earth for his food
With stone for building His churches
And trees for making His rood.
There where the white light flickers,
Our Creator is with us yet,
To be worshipped by you and the woman
Of the slacks and the cigarette.

* * * * *

The great door shuts, and lessens
That roar of churchyard trees
And the Presence of God Incarnate
Has brought me to my knees.
'I acknowledge my transgressions'
The well-known phrases rolled
With thunder sailing over
From the heavenly clouded wold.
'And my sin is ever before me.'
There in the lighted East
He stood in that lowering sunlight,
An Indian Christian priest.

And why he was here in Lincolnshire
I neither asked nor knew,
Nor whether his flock was many
Nor whether his flock was few
I thought of the heaving waters
That bore him from sun glare harsh
Of some Indian Anglican Mission
To this green enormous marsh.
There where the white light flickers,
Here, as the rains descend,
The same mysterious Godhead
Is welcoming His friend.

4

The Church in Society

4 The Church in Society

To John Betjeman, the Church was undoubtedly the most significant institution in England. When he wrote about the Church, he was to his way of thinking also writing of England. As he wrote in the poem 'Churchyards', 'Our churches are our history shown / In wood and glass and iron and stone.' The range of what Betjeman has to say about the Church is broad indeed. He writes of the Church's architectural and liturgical beauty, of its role as the storehouse of English history and tradition, of its symbolic locus as the centre of the community and its function as a central source of cultural identity for the English people. What a fearsome thing it was for Betjeman to consider the decline of the Church. It saddened him to witness not only a national loss of faith but what he perceived to be a broader decline of English culture as well. For Betjeman, the Church encouraged and sustained his faith during times of doubt, but its social role was also significant for him. In the Church of England, Betjeman found beauty, a sense of community and a space for history and tradition to dwell.

No poem of John Betjeman's captures the complementary traits of beauty, community and history in the Church of England better than 'St Saviour's, Aberdeen Park, Highbury, London, N.' The geographic specificity of the title reminds us that the Church of England is not simply a national institution, but the centre of parish life even in urban and suburban London neighbourhoods. Much of the poem emphasizes the church's undying 'polychromatic' beauty in the midst of a parish that has undergone a massive demographic change. Once the proud parish church for affluent Victorians and Edwardians, by the 1940s Highbury St Saviour's sat in an area of blight and waste. Betjeman uses the contrast between the church's lovely past and its current state of abandonment to comment on the decline of community in postwar Britain and the concomitant lack of interest in beauty and tradition. This is an elegiac lament not just for a waning church but a culture as well. The church's interior opulence, in contrast with its declining parish, gives the poet hope that the spiritual life of his nation is not yet dead; revisiting communal history, he walks softly 'Over these same encaustics' that his parents once walked and reflects on the relationship between religion and culture. In the chancel of this church fated for redundancy, the pulsing heart of God continues to beat, softly but relentlessly opposing the persistent chaos and detritus of human and mechanical noise, the physical and aural litter of modern existence. God's 'throbbing heart' is immanent in this church, in the reserved Eucharistic sacrament; although it is the primary function of the 'Bread so white and small' to save souls, not to solve sociological problems, the poet's devotion to the Eucharist is a vital part of a complex of attitudes that includes an awareness of beauty, a respect for the past and a grievous sense of an England slipping forever away: an England of faith, of communal tradition, of aesthetic power. Thus when he collapses at the high altar in St Saviour's, the poet is petitioning God for the salvation of his own soul as well as the collective soul of his nation.

Like 'St Saviour's, Aberdeen Park', the rest of the poems in this chapter emphasize the social function of the established Church and symbolize it as the locus for all that should be celebrated or lamented in Betjeman's England. The central emphasis of the first three of these poems is the aesthetic beauty of the Church of England. 'Bristol' is a tribute to the art of bell-ringing, an activity that does so much more than summon believers to worship. It rouses a blend of melancholy and joy within those fortunate enough to be outside when the bells begin to ring.

'Bristol' associates the peal of church bells with all that is beautiful in English towns and countryside, and the poem's setting in the aftermath of a gentle rain suggests the sensation of purity and restoration that accompanies the lovely flood of music. The beauty of Anglo-Catholic worship is the focus of 'Holy Trinity, Sloane Street'. A poem whose baroque solemnity reflects both the architecture and the liturgy of its namesake church, this is the most lush and mysterious of Betjeman's religious poems. Candles and incense, iconic decorations and penitential liturgy fill the poem, which describes a religious experience bordering upon the sexual. A perhaps more emotionally restrained expression of this mystery can be found in another poem celebrating Anglican tradition. Set in what may be the most architecturally perfect and pleasing chapel in England, 'Sunday Morning, King's Cambridge' uses a blaze of colour to depict the sincerest efforts of man appropriately to worship the divine. Abiding faith is here fused with a deep appreciation of both architectural and natural beauty. The result is a tribute to the splendour of Anglican worship. Although the poem admits that the divine is not found exclusively in the structures of man's design, the magnificent late-medieval chapel of King's College is undoubtedly a dwelling-place of God and is therefore the poem's most important symbol for God's strength and presence. The chapel's stunning fan-vaulted ceiling, a wonder of fifteenth-century engineering, needs no buttress beyond the metaphorical buttress of common prayer, the recitation of which unites the English people across the ages and with eternity. The living and the dead, the choir and the poet, all join in an eternal praise of God; through the seeming timelessness of Anglican common prayer, they approximate the timelessness of eternity itself.

The community of believers united by Anglican common prayer is a central theme of many of Betjeman's poems. Many of them are built, like 'Bristol', around the magnificent aural image of church bells. In 'Verses Turned', the peal of a single church bell draws an entire parish into both social and spiritual communion. The poem emphasizes that even obscure, remote or forgotten churches are significant: as a village is a microcosm of the nation, so a parish history recounts the history of England. The 'plaintive bell' of St Katherine's, Chiselhampton, is a plea to save both this little parish church and the national Church as well. A community across time is created by the activity of bell-ringing in 'On Hearing the Full Peal of Ten Bells from Christ Church, Swindon, Wilts'. Here, bell-ringing unites past, present and future generations, despite the disruptive effects of modern technology. 'Village Wedding' blends imagery of natural beauty, a rain-purified atmosphere, church bells and a festive occasion that spans the generations. It seems as if the entire parish of Uffington is brought together into the ancient church to witness a sacrament that binds together not just a young couple but all the living and dead with the timeless communal rituals of Christian faith. 'Church of England Thoughts' describes how a ringing of bells reminds the poet of the various forms of Anglican worship. Such divisions and distinctions are insignificant, however, as worshippers are united by a 'multiplicity of bells'. Since these are collegiate rather than church bells, however, there is an ambiguous note; as the peal dissipates, the poet is dragged into the harsh reality of a modern society antipathetic to the capacity for communal regeneration the Church of England offers.

The potential for communal bonds to form by means of Anglican tradition and common worship represented for Betjeman the best way for a people to preserve its culture and history. As the ambiguity of 'St Saviour's, Aberdeen Park' and 'Church of England Thoughts' reveals, Betjeman is preoccupied by an anxiety that tradition and community will be lost as the Church slips into decline. Thus we detect an almost insistent litany that community must somehow be restored even when churches are lost. In 'City' the poet imagines himself sitting in the churchyard of St Botolph's, Bishopsgate, where the tolling bell and waft of incense awaken memories of past generations. As in 'In Willesden Churchyard', the elements of worship are experienced in the churchyard rather than the church, and the service awakens only ghosts. Betjeman's concern about the dying Church would grow more intense after the war when so many of London's churches, especially in the City, were pulled down because of bomb damage and demographic change to make room for office buildings. 'Monody on the Death of Aldersgate Street Station', which seems to memorialize the steam-train era, has as its parallel focus the end of the era of faith, symbolized by the double loss of both Victorian railway stations and City churches. Here the waning of the Church is given specifically social causes and effects. Betjeman recites a litany of churches lost or threatened, their names, syllabically metrical and quaintly monickered, rolling poetically off his tongue. The poem laments the missing sound of their church bells as yet a further instance of cultural and communal loss, like gaslights and steam engines. The transformation of the City into London's financial district, with all its alien and technological improvements, disrupts and sunders what once was a vibrant community of tradition and ritual. What 'Monody' accomplishes with a lament, 'Distant View of a Provincial Town' does with wit. The poem humorously implies that trains as much as churches can take you on a spiritual journey; the amusing claim that we can be redeemed by a railway suggests that the redemption Betjeman has in mind is cultural rather than spiritual and that this can be accomplished as well by steam as by faith, by God's Wonderful Railway or by the Eucharist. The equation between the GWR and the C of E suggests that a similar fate is in store for both; as Betjeman lamented the scheme to nationalize the railway, so would he also have lamented any effort to disestablish the national Church. The communal nature of parishes within a national Church is the point of 'Septuagesima', a serious poem in light verse that praises the humble parishioners all over England whose strenuous efforts sustain village churches and thus the established Church.

The preservation of the Church and of churches was clearly central in the imagination of John Betjeman, but he could never separate his devotion to the Church of England from his devotion both to the architecture of man's creating and to the nature of God's creating. This is the central premise of 'Sunday Afternoon Service in St Enodoc Church, Cornwall', a long poem in which Betjeman describes himself, summoned by a single bell, hastening past tidal pools and across sand dunes to attend a service of Evensong in an ancient, remote and almost forgotten parish church. As his mind wanders through the service and out across the lushness of coastal Cornwall, he experiences God both within and without the church as the liturgical offices of the Book of Common Prayer conflate with the wildness of the Cornish landscape. Perhaps this is a lingering element of Celtic mysticism, for in this service of Evening Prayer Betjeman is reminded that God is alive in this world and that he himself is an integral part of the vital history of God's creation. In this poem, Betjeman discovers a community and a tradition much larger than England's. This is the community of all believers. Despite its vulnerability to the elements, humanity has for centuries relied on the incarnate God for hope, security and the promise of eternity. The simple truths of Christianity which bind believers across time and space are rendered by Betjeman's poem in stark profundity. In this poem, beauty, community and tradition all transcend the limitations of culture.

St Saviour's, Aberdeen Park, Highbury, London, N.[1]

With oh such peculiar branching and over-reaching of wire
  Trolley-bus standards pick their threads from the London
    sky
Diminishing up the perspective, Highbury-bound retire
  Threads and buses and standards with plane trees volleying
    by
And, more peculiar still, that ever-increasing spire
  Bulges over the housetops, polychromatic and high.

Stop the trolley-bus, stop! And here, where the roads unite
  Of weariest worn-out London—no cigarettes, no beer,
No repairs undertaken, nothing in stock—alight;
  For over the waste of willow-herb, look at her, sailing clear,
A great Victorian church, tall, unbroken and bright
  In a sun that's setting in Willesden and saturating us here.

These were the streets my parents knew when they loved and
    won—
  The brougham that crunched the gravel, the laurel-girt paths
    that wind,
Geranium-beds for the lawn, Venetian blinds for the sun,
  A separate tradesman's entrance, straw in the mews behind,
Just in the four-mile radius where hackney carriages run,
  Solid Italianate houses for the solid commercial mind.

---

[1] St Saviour's was built in 1865–6 in the decorated style of the Arts and Crafts movement. Betjeman's parents were married there in 1902. After a long decline, St Saviour's was declared redundant and closed in 1981. Since 1988 it has been leased to the Florence Trust Studios, which support young artists.

These were the streets they knew; and I, by descent, belong
  To these tall neglected houses divided into flats.
Only the church remains, where carriages used to throng
  And my mother stepped out in flounces and my father
    stepped out in spats
To shadowy stained-glass matins or gas-lit evensong
  And back in a country quiet with doffing of chimney hats.

Great red church of my parents, cruciform crossing they knew—
  Over these same encaustics they and their parents trod
Round through a red-brick transept for a once familiar pew
  Where the organ set them singing and the sermon let them nod
And up this coloured brickwork the same long shadows grew
  As these in the stencilled chancel where I kneel in the presence
    of God.

Wonder beyond Time's wonders, that Bread so white and small
  Veiled in golden curtains, too mighty for men to see,
Is the Power which sends the shadows up this polychrome wall,
  Is God who created the present, the chain-smoking millions
    and me;
Beyond the throb of the engines is the throbbing heart of all—
  Christ, at this Highbury altar, I offer myself To Thee.

Bristol

Green upon the flooded Avon shone the after-storm-wet-sky
Quick the struggling withy branches let the leaves of autumn fly
And a star shone over Bristol, wonderfully far and high.

Ringers in an oil-lit belfry—Bitton? Kelston?[1] who shall say?—
Smoothly practising a plain course, caverned out the dying day
As their melancholy music flooded up and ebbed away.

Then all Somerset was round me and I saw the clippers ride,
High above the moonlit houses, triple-masted on the tide,
By the tall embattled church-towers of the Bristol waterside.

And an undersong to branches dripping into pools and wells
Out of multitudes of elm trees over leagues of hills and dells
Was the mathematic pattern of a plain course on the bells.*

```
*1 2 2 4 4 5 5 3 3 1 1
 2 1 4 2 5 4 3 5 1 3 2
 3 4 1 5 2 3 4 1 5 2 3
 4 3 5 1 3 2 1 4 2 5 4
 5 5 3 3 1 1 2 2 4 4 5
```

Holy Trinity, Sloane Street

MCMVII

An Acolyte singeth
Light six white tapers with the Flame of Art,
Send incense wreathing to the lily flowers,
And, with your cool hands white,
Swing the warm censer round my bruised heart,
Drop, dove-grey eyes, your penitential showers
On this pale acolyte.

A confirmandus continueth
The tall red house soars upward to the stars,
The doors are chased with sardonyx and gold,
And in the long white room
Thin drapery draws backward to unfold
Cadogan Square between the window-bars
And Whistler's mother knitting in the gloom.

The Priest endeth
How many hearts turn Motherward to-day?
(Red roses faint not on your twining stems!)
Bronze triptych doors unswing!
Wait, restive heart, wait, rounded lips, to pray,
Mid beaten copper interset with gems
Behold! Behold! your King!

Sunday Morning, King's Cambridge

File into yellow candle light, fair choristers of King's
  Lost in the shadowy silence of canopied Renaissance stalls
In blazing glass above the dark glow skies and thrones and
    wings
  Blue, ruby, gold and green between the whiteness of the walls
And with what rich precision the stonework soars and springs
  To fountain out a spreading vault—a shower that never falls.

The white of windy Cambridge courts, the cobbles brown and
    dry,
  The gold of plaster Gothic with ivy overgrown,
The apple-red, the silver fronts, the wide green flats and high,
  The yellowing elm-trees circled out on islands of their own—
Oh, here behold all colours change that catch the flying sky
  To waves of pearly light that heave along the shafted stone.

In far East Anglian churches, the clasped hands lying long
  Recumbent on sepulchral slabs or effigied in brass
Buttress with prayer this vaulted roof so white and light and
    strong
  And countless congregations as the generations pass
Join choir and great crowned organ case, in centuries of song
  To praise Eternity contained in Time and coloured glass.

Verses Turned
in Aid of a Public Subscription (1952)
towards the restoration of the
Church of St. Katherine
Chiselhampton, Oxon[1]

Across the wet November night
The church is bright with candlelight
   And waiting Evensong.
A single bell with plaintive strokes
Pleads louder than the stirring oaks
   The leafless lanes along.

It calls the choirboys from their tea
And villagers, the two or three,
   Damp down the kitchen fire,
Let out the cat, and up the lane
Go paddling through the gentle rain
   Of misty Oxfordshire.

How warm the many candles shine
On SAMUEL DOWBIGGIN'S design
   For this interior neat,
These high box pews of Georgian days
Which screen us from the public gaze
   When we make answer meet;

How gracefully their shadow falls
On bold pilasters down the walls

---

[1] An eighteenth-century church now preserved by the Churches Conservation Trust.

And on the pulpit high.
The chandeliers would twinkle gold
    As pre-Tractarian sermons roll'd
        Doctrinal, sound and dry.

From that west gallery no doubt
The viol and serpent tooted out
    The Tallis tune to Ken,[1]
And firmly at the end of prayers
The clerk below the pulpit stairs
    Would thunder out 'Amen'.

But every wand'ring thought will cease
Before the noble altarpiece
    With carven swags array'd,
For there in letters all may read
The Lord's Commandments, Prayer and Creed,
    And decently display'd.

On country mornings sharp and clear
The penitent in faith draw near
    And kneeling here below
Partake the Heavenly Banquet spread
Of Sacramental Wine and Bread
    And JESUS' presence know.

And must that plaintive bell in vain
Plead loud along the dripping lane?
    And must the building fall?
Not while we love the Church and live
And of our charity will give
    Our much, our more, our all.

---

[1] The hymn to which Betjeman refers is probably 'All praise to Thee, my God, this night'. Thomas Tallis (*c.* 1505–85) was the chief composer of church music in the Tudor era. Thomas Ken (1637–1711), bishop, was the author of the hymn popularly known as the 'Doxology'.

On Hearing the Full Peal of Ten Bells from Christ Church, Swindon, Wilts.

Your peal of ten ring over then this town,
Ring on my men nor ever ring them down.
This winter chill, let sunset spill cold fire
On villa'd hill and on Sir Gilbert's[1] spire,
So new, so high, so pure, so broach'd, so tall.
Long run the thunder of the bells through all!

Oh still white headstones on these fields of sound
Hear you the wedding joybells wheeling round?
Oh brick-built breeding boxes of new souls,
Hear how the pealing through the louvres rolls!
Now birth and death-reminding bells ring clear,
Loud under 'planes and over changing gear.

---

[1] Sir George Gilbert Scott (1811–78) was the most prominent architect of the nineteenth-century Gothic revival.

Village Wedding

In summer wind the elm leaves sing,
    And sharp's the shade they're shedding,
And loud and soft the church bells ring
    For Sally Weaver's wedding.[1]

With chasing light the meadows fill,
    The greenness growing greener,
As racing over White Horse Hill
    Come bluer skies and cleaner.

The chalk-white walls, the steaming thatch
    In rain-washed air are clearing,
And waves of sunshine run to catch
    The bride for her appearing.

Inside the church in every pew
    Sit old friends, older grown now;
Their children whom our children knew
    Have children of their own now.

The babies wail, the organ plays,
    Now thunderous, now lighter;
The brighter day of Sally's days
    Grows every moment brighter.

And all the souls of Uffington,
    The dead among the living,
Seem witnessing the rite begun
    Of taking and of giving.

---

[1] Sally Weaver had been the best friend of Candida, the Betjemans' daughter.

The flying clouds! The flying years!
  This church of centuries seven!
How new its weathered stone appears
  When vows are made in Heaven!

Church of England Thoughts
occasioned by hearing the bells of Magdalen Tower from the Botanic Garden, Oxford on St. Mary Magdalen's Day

I see the urn against the yew,
    The sunlit urn of sculptured stone,
I see its shapely shadow fall
On this enormous garden wall
    Which makes a kingdom of its own.

A grassy kingdom sweet to view
    With tiger lilies still in flower
And beds of umbelliferae
Ranged in Linnaean symmetry,
    All in the sound of Magdalen Tower.

A multiplicity of bells,
    A changing cadence, rich and deep
Swung from those pinnacles on high
To fill the trees and flood the sky
    And rock the sailing clouds to sleep.

A Church of England sound, it tells
    Of 'moderate' worship, God and State,
Where matins congregations go
Conservative and good and slow
    To elevations of the plate.

And loud through resin-scented chines
    And purple rhododendrons roll'd,
I hear the bells for Eucharist
From churches blue with incense mist
    Where reredoses twinkle gold.

Chapels-of-ease by railway lines
    And humble streets and smells of gas
I hear your plaintive ting-tangs call
From many a gabled western wall
    To Morning Prayer or Holy Mass.

In country churches old and pale
    I hear the changes smoothly rung
And watch the coloured sallies fly
From rugged hands to rafters high
    As round and back the bells are swung.

Before the spell begin to fail,
    Before the bells have lost their power,
Before the grassy kingdom fade
And Oxford traffic roar invade,
    I thank the bells of Magdalen Tower.

City

When the great bell
BOOMS over the Portland stone urn, and
From the carved cedar wood
Rises the odour of incense,
I SIT DOWN
In St. Botolph Bishopsgate Churchyard
And wait for the spirit of my grandfather
Toddling along from the Barbican.

Monody on the Death of
Aldersgate Street Station

Snow falls in the buffet of Aldersgate station,
  Soot hangs in the tunnel in clouds of steam.
City of London! before the next desecration
  Let your steepled forest of churches be my theme.

Sunday Silence! with every street a dead street,
  Alley and courtyard empty and cobbled mews,
Till 'tingle tang' the bell of St Mildred's Bread Street
  Summoned the sermon taster to high box pews,

And neighbouring towers and spirelets joined the ringing
  With answering echoes from heavy commercial walls
Till all were drowned as the sailing clouds went singing
  On the roaring flood of a twelve-voiced peal from Paul's.

Then would the years fall off and Thames run slowly;
  Out into marshy meadow-land flowed the Fleet:
And the walled-in City of London, smelly and holy,
  Had a tinkling mass house in every cavernous street.

The bells rang down and St Michael Paternoster
  Would take me into its darkness from College Hill,
Or Christ Church Newgate Street (with St Leonard Foster)
  Would be late for Mattins and ringing insistent still.[1]

---

[1] St Michael Paternoster Royal still stands, but St Mildred's and Christ Church
(excepting its tower) were destroyed in the Blitz.

Last of the east wall sculpture, a cherub gazes
  On broken arches, rosebay, bracken and dock,
Where once I heard the roll of the Prayer Book phrases
  And the sumptuous tick of the old west gallery clock.

Snow falls in the buffet of Aldersgate station,
  Toiling and doomed from Moorgate Street puffs the train,
For us of the steam and the gas-light, the lost generation,
  The new white cliffs of the City are built in vain.

Distant View of a Provincial Town

Beside those spires so spick and span
    Against an unencumbered sky
The old Great Western Railway ran
    When someone different was I.

St Aidan's with the prickly nobs
    And iron spikes and coloured tiles—
Where Auntie Maud devoutly bobs
    In those enriched vermilion aisles:

St George's where the mattins bell
    But rarely drowned the trams for prayer—
No Popish sight or sound or smell
    Disturbed that gas-invaded air:

St Mary's where the Rector preached
    In such a jolly friendly way
On cricket, football, things that reached
    The simple life of every day:

And that United Benefice
    With entrance permanently locked,—
How Gothic, grey and sad it is
    Since Mr Grogley was unfrocked!

The old Great Western Railway shakes
    The old Great Western Railway spins—
The old Great Western Railway makes
    Me very sorry for my sins.

Septuagesima

Septuagesima—seventy days
To Easter's primrose tide of praise;
The Gesimas[1]—Septua, Sexa, Quinc
Mean Lent is near, which makes you think.
Septuagesima—when we're told
To 'run the race', to 'keep our hold',
Ignore injustice, not give in,
And practise stern self-discipline;
A somewhat unattractive time
Which hardly lends itself to rhyme.
    But still it gives the chance to me
To praise our dear old C. of E.
So other Churches please forgive
Lines on the Church in which I live,
The Church of England of my birth,
The kindest Church to me on earth.
There may be those who like things fully
Argued out, and call you 'woolly';
Ignoring Creeds and Catechism
They say the C. of E.'s 'in schism'.
There may be those who much resent
Priest, Liturgy, and Sacrament,
Whose worship is what they call 'free',
Well, let them be so, but for me
There's refuge in the C. of E.
And when it comes that I must die
I hope the Vicar's standing by,
I won't care if he's 'Low' or 'High'

---

[1]   The Sundays before Lent.

For he'll be there to aid my soul
On that dread journey to its goal,
With Sacrament and prayer and Blessing
After I've done my last confessing.
And at that time may I receive
The Grace most firmly to believe,
For if the Christian's Faith's untrue
What is the point of me and you?
    But this is all anticipating
Septuagesima—time of waiting,
Running the race or holding fast.
Let's praise the man who goes to light
The church stove on an icy night.
Let's praise that hard-worked he or she
The Treasurer of the P.C.C.
Let's praise the cleaner of the aisles,
The nave and candlesticks and tiles.
Let's praise the organist who tries
To make the choir increase in size,
Or if that simply cannot be,
Just to improve its quality.
Let's praise the ringers in the tower
Who come to ring in cold and shower.
But most of all let's praise the few
Who are seen in their accustomed pew
Throughout the year, whate'er the weather,
That they may worship God together.
These, like a fire of glowing coals,
Strike warmth into each other's souls,
And though they be but two or three
They keep the Church for you and me.

Sunday Afternoon Service in St Enodoc Church, Cornwall

Come on! come on! This hillock hides the spire,
Now that one and now none. As winds about
The burnished path through lady's finger, thyme
And bright varieties of saxifrage,
So grows the tinny tenor faint or loud
And all things draw towards St Enodoc.

Come on! come on! and it is five to three.

Paths, unfamiliar to golfers' brogues,
Cross the eleventh fairway broadside on
And leave the fourteenth tee for thirteenth green,
Ignoring Royal and Ancient, bound for God.
    Come on! come on! no longer bare of foot,
The sole grows hot in London shoes again.
Jack Lambourne in his Sunday navy-blue
Wears tie and collar, all from Selfridge's.
There's Enid with a silly parasol,
And Graham in gray flannel with a crease
Across the middle of his coat which lay
Pressed 'neath the box of his Meccano set,
Sunday to Sunday.
    Still, Come on! come on!
The tinny tenor. Hover-flies remain
More than a moment on a ragwort bunch,
And people's passing shadows don't disturb
Red Admirals basking with their wings apart.
    A mile of sunny, empty sand away,
A mile of shallow pools and lugworm casts,
Safe, faint and surfy, laps the lowest tide.
    Even the villas have a Sunday look.

The Ransom mower's locked into the shed.
'I have a splitting headache from the sun,'
And bedroom windows flutter cheerful chintz
Where, double-aspirined, a mother sleeps;
While father in the loggia reads a book,
Large, desultory, birthday-present size,
Published with coloured plates by *Country Life*,
A Bernard Darwin on *The English Links*
Or Braid and Taylor on *The Mashie Shot*.
Come on! come on! he thinks of Monday's round—
Come on! come on! that interlocking grip!
Come on! come on! he drops into a doze—
Come on! come on! more far and far away
The children climb a final stile to church;
Electoral Roll still flapping in the porch—
Then the cool silence of St Enodoc.

My eyes, recovering in the sudden shade,
Discern the long-known little things within—
A map of France in damp above my pew,
Grey-blue of granite in the small arcade
(Late Perp: and not a Parker specimen
But roughly hewn on windy Bodmin Moor),
The modest windows palely glazed with green,
The smooth slate floor, the rounded wooden roof,
The Norman arch, the cable-moulded font—
All have a humble and West Country look.
Oh 'drastic restoration' of the guide!
Oh three-light window by a Plymouth firm!
Absurd, truncated screen! oh sticky pews!
Embroidered altar-cloth! untended lamps!
So soaked in worship you are loved too well
For that dispassionate and critic stare
That I would use beyond the parish bounds
Biking in high-banked lanes from tower to tower

On sunny, antiquarian afternoons.
    Come on! come on! a final pull. Tom Blake
Stalks over from the bell-rope to his pew
Just as he slopes about the windy cliffs
Looking for wreckage in a likely tide,
Nor gives the Holy Table glance or nod.
A rattle as red baize is drawn aside,
Miss Rhoda Poulden pulls the tremolo,
The oboe, flute and vox humana stops;
A Village Voluntary fills the air
And ceases suddenly as it began,
Save for one oboe faintly humming on,
As slow the weary clergyman subsides
Tired with his bike-ride from the parish church.
He runs his hands once, twice, across his face
'Dearly beloved ...' and a bumble-bee
Zooms itself free into the churchyard sun
And so my thoughts this happy Sabbathtide.
    Where deep cliffs loom enormous, where cascade
Mesembryanthemum and stone-crop down,
Where the gull looks no larger than a lark
Hung midway twixt the cliff-top and the sand,
Sun-shadowed valleys roll along the sea.
Forced by the backwash, see the nearest wave
Rise to a wall of huge, translucent green
And crumble into spray along the top
Blown seaward by the land-breeze. Now she breaks
And in an arch of thunder plunges down
To burst and tumble, foam on top of foam,
Criss-crossing, baffled, sucked and shot again,
A waterfall of whiteness, down a rock,
Without a source but roller's furthest reach:
And tufts of sea-pink, high and dry for years,
Are flooded out of ledges, boulders seem
No bigger than a pebble washed about

In this tremendous tide. Oh kindly slate!
To give me shelter in this crevice dry.
These shivering stalks of bent-grass, lucky plant,
Have better chance than I to last the storm.
Oh kindly slate of these unaltered cliffs,
Firm, barren substrate of our windy fields!
Oh lichened slate in walls, they knew your worth
Who raised you up to make this House of God
What faith was his, that dim, that Cornish saint,
Small rushlight of a long-forgotten church,
Who lived with God on this unfriendly shore,
Who knew He made the Atlantic and the stones
And destined seamen here to end their lives
Dashed on a rock, rolled over in the surf,
And not one hair forgotten. Now they lie
In centuries of sand beside the church.
Less pitiable are they than the corpse
Of a large golfer, only four weeks dead,
This sunlit and sea-distant afternoon.
'Praise ye the Lord!' and in another key
The Lord's name by harmonium be praised.
'The Second Evening and the Fourteenth Psalm.'

5

Vanity and Hypocrisy in the Church

5 Vanity and Hypocrisy
in the Church

Although John Betjeman loved the Church of England dearly, he was not blind to its faults. The poems in this chapter all take the Church to task for its self-satisfaction and spiritual blindness. They reveal the tendency toward snobbery, smugness and hypocrisy among both clergy and parishioners; and they excoriate the Church for its obsession with its own beauty, ritual, history and privilege. Despite the implication that the Church often failed abjectly, Betjeman rarely loses his sense of humour, and none of these poems is marked by outright rage. However, they reveal the emotional range of which he was capable, from bitterness to sorrow to playful banter. He also reveals a range of poetic voices; while some of these poems embody his own voice, many are built upon a distinct persona who betrays vanity or hypocrisy in his or her own words while ironically thinking that he or she is both spiritually and socially admirable. Betjeman is not normally regarded as a satirist, perhaps these poems suggest that he was, albeit a fairly gentle one.

The first group of poems addresses not individuals or parishes but institutional problems within the Church of England. The first three poems in particular satirize the tendency of the Church to take its buildings for granted and, ignoring both the delicate nature of ecclesiastical architecture and the fundamental function of these buildings as spaces to foster the worship of God, to alter their aesthetics to suit the tastes and needs of the present without consideration of past and future. 'Hymn' is a rousing assault on the widespread and drastic 'restorations' of ancient churches during the Victorian era. As a parodic echo of the familiar hymn, 'The Church's One Foundation', Betjeman's poem implies that the Victorian effort to create a hegemonic neo-Gothic ecclesiastical architecture resulted in widespread defilement of historic sites of worship. His tone is scathing, as the speaker in his poem grows deliriously idolatrous toward the new face of the church; such restorations are wrong because they distract the worshipper from praising God. 'Electric Light and Heating' focuses not on restoration but modernization. Parishioners' complaints about their comfort have led to the addition of bulbs, pipes, wires, boxes and so forth all over the church, defiling every feature from steeple to pulpit to decorated wall. Betjeman blames parishioners who are too lazy to maintain ancient heating and lighting systems. He may appear silly or obsessive to us in his opposition to modern technology, but to him the innovations constitute 'shameful' appendages because they 'rob our church of mystery' and are aesthetically unpleasing. 'The Friends of the Cathedral' uses the device of the rhetorical question to expose the vanity and blindness afflicting an organization responsible for maintaining the great English cathedrals. The questions go unanswered within the poem, but the reader can easily supply the responses. Although the cathedral's 'Friends' are well-intentioned, all their efforts are directed toward meeting the needs of tourists and tour guides, not those of worshippers. It is the 'Friends' who have added a children's corner to a shrine, added chairs and ashtrays for the assistants, hung explanatory signs on monuments for visitors and wired the cathedral for the obnoxious echoing speakers. The poem wonders what sort of friendship a cathedral truly needs.

The next two poems also address issues of architectural vanity within the Church of England, but in distinct and unusual ways, both of them suggesting disparate paths in which the Church has lost its direction. 'Not Necessarily

Leeds' is a poem occasioned by the efforts of the Church of England in the 1950s to sell off churches deemed redundant. After the Bishop of London sold St Peter's, Great Windmill Street, Betjeman was determined to prevent further disaster, and in this poem first published in *The Spectator* he attacks the Bishop of Ripon and the Archdeacon of Leeds for their plan to demolish Holy Trinity, Leeds, and sell the land. Though perhaps tempted to defend the church on grounds of historic and architectural merit, Betjeman relies on a more powerful appeal, attacking the bishop for following demographic trends instead of evangelizing. The bishop, motivated not so much by greed as by an obsession with financial stability, is all too happy to close an urban parish with declining attendance and create a united benefice if that will keep his budget in the black. Betjeman's attack on the bishop's apparent apathy to the spiritual needs of an urban, postwar people worked, and the church was not closed. Using the same unusual metrical pattern of dactylic tetrameter, 'St Barnabas, Oxford' adopts the unlikely approach of satirizing the Church for building unnecessary churches and for being more interested in displaying ecclesiastical beauty and power than in noticing the natural beauty that such churches displace. 'St Barnabas, Oxford' describes a church whose 'polychromatical' splendour is matched by the aural and visual spectacle of its Anglo-Catholic liturgy. However, the beauty of St Barnabas has come with a price. While bells may add to the beauty of an English setting, a church, particularly an edifice of such grandeur, may in fact detract from its surroundings. Thus Betjeman suggests that this Byzantine monolith has displaced the beauty of an English meadow, the sort that inspired Romantic poets. The manmade has supplanted the natural beauty of the England that God created. In fact, Betjeman implies that church often distracts the worshipper from God. Not only has man destroyed God's creation with a grand and haughty monument to the worship of God, but he has also cut himself off from his source of creativity. In a vein of Romantic effusion, Betjeman implies that the best place to find God – as to find poetic inspiration – is in a temple of God's making, not man's; in a meadow, not in a church. In both of these poems, the vanity of the Church is not merely its pride but also its futility and blindness.

The next group of poems addresses with relatively gentle satire the typical problems that plague parish life within the Church of England: a clergy distracted or tempted by secular matters; apathy and laziness that makes a parish wither; and parishes split by unresolved social conflicts. 'Exchange of Livings' is an unusual poem: parodying classified newspaper advertisements in which clergy attempt to trade their incumbencies, Betjeman seizes the opportunity to expose the motivations lurking behind such desires for clerical change. The reasons of course have nothing to do with spiritual growth: such parsons are looking for a change of scenery and the chance to spend more time away from their churches. 'Blame the Vicar' is just as light-hearted in tone, but here Betjeman sympathizes with vicars who might desire to exchange their livings. He describes the unrelenting pressures parishioners heap upon their priests: to set an example in virtue; to be a comfort by not discussing such unseemly topics as hell; to keep everyone happy and cheerful; to heal parish rifts; and never ever to give offence. What parishioners want from their priest amounts to an impossible paradox. They want him to be both morally superior and yet to embody humility; they put him on a pedestal only to knock him off. A poem in a similar vein is 'Parochial Church Council', which explores the viciousness of parish leaders who serve on their local PCC, particularly when dealing with finances and matters of liturgical style. Much of the satire works by comparing ecclesial and governmental administrative structures. Betjeman's irony is simple; though he is direct about parish hypocrisy, his tone remains relatively genial. Taken together, 'Parochial Church Council' and 'Blame the Vicar' suggest that if we expect tolerance and even indulgence for our hypocrisies, then we should at least stop demanding so much from our priests. Lack of tolerance as the most common form of ecclesiastical hypocrisy is the central theme in 'Diary of a Church Mouse'. The poem's speaker is a mouse who resides in a church 'among long-discarded cassocks / Damp stools and half-split hassocks'. Although it seems a devout and harmless creature, gradually a darker side is revealed. The mouse observes its parish's annual Harvest Festival and uses the occasion to speak badly of other mice who show up only for special events. Unbaptized and agnostic rodents have no business here, and the mouse wants them to go away. The rich mice only come to hear the music and have no interest in supporting the parish. The mouse wishes to exclude all mice who don't measure up to its own standard of Christian observance; to its way of thinking, if you do not come every Sunday then you should not come for feastdays and special services. Finally, Betjeman has the mouse wish that rodents could be as devoutly religious as humans. His solutions to all these complex parish problems are simple, but that is because Christ's message was simple: spend time in prayer, observe the sacraments and demonstrate charity.

In the last group of poems, Betjeman shifts his focus from general problems in the Church and in parishes to individuals, and as a consequence his tone grows more censorious. Each of these poems captures the voice of a hypocrite and, excepting the first one, each speaker is blind to his or her spiritual hubris. 'Guilt' begins with the familiar imagery of a soot-blanketed London rendered as an urban hell. The speaker has abandoned faith and hope, but confessing to himself his dishonesty he hides his faithlessness behind a 'breastplate of self-righteousness'. The more particularized portraits in the last three poems have a persona oblivious to his or her hypocrisy that is revealed through the irony of a Browningesque dramatic monologue.

'Bristol and Clifton' is set in a church after a service of Evening Prayer. The speaker is showing off a stained-glass window dedicated to his late wife, but any sympathy that this situation creates in the reader evaporates quickly as we sense his vanity and hypocrisy. To the speaker, the church is an opportunity to glorify not simply his wife's memory but his own, who commissioned the window, and a parade of vanities progresses from this point to the end of the poem. As people's warden, the speaker, who fears and loathes high church ritual, has had new radiators installed so as to prevent any future construction of altars. He despises kneeling and genuflection, and wants the only ritual to be the taking of the offering. When his interlocutor spots a lone woman still praying in the church and suggests they take the conversation outside, the speaker dismisses her as some sort of alien Catholic who needs to be hastened out since the service has ended. The poem ends just as abruptly, and we are left with the statement that the church should be locked up and the lights turned out. A more apt symbol for the coldly hypocritical heart could not be found than the action of locking the door and extinguishing the light.

In 'St Mary Magdalen, Old Fish Street Hill', Betjeman's persona is proud of being rector's warden, though the church has so dwindled in numbers that it is beyond help. The speaker blames aesthetics for the decline, namely the plain and uninspiring design of Christopher Wren who rebuilt the church after the Great Fire. Although elsewhere Betjeman would admit that there is a significant link between aesthetics and faith, in this poem the decline of St Mary Magdalen is attributed to a blend of demography, snobbery and politics. For years the ranks of the church's congregation were filled with non-tithing poor children, but as they were not the most desirable congregation the church's oligarchs shunted them off to the balcony until a diocesan or parochial committee could simply make them disappear. The rector's warden does not know where they have gone and does not seem to understand why this has dealt such a mortal blow to his church. Oblivious to demographics, the speaker is unable to grasp the significance of the City's dramatically falling population and its sad plethora of empty churches; equally he fails to fathom that the community of charity children had been St Mary Magdalen's only community, and now there is none. Snobbery and blindness have been the death of this church.

The masterpiece of Betjeman's satirical poems is 'In Westminster Abbey'. This is set during the Blitz, and is an indictment of churchgoing hypocrisy. The poem's persona has entered the abbey to pray for a moment before hurrying off to a social engagement. She is a chauvinist, racist and snob who, conflating spiritual and material treasures, is most concerned with how the war will affect her portfolio. She blithely believes that doing her duty in the war effort honours Christ's injunctions, and her nationalism leads her to ask the Lord himself to 'bomb the Germans'. Proud of what she perceives as humility, she will gladly forgive God if he accidentally and incompetently kills a few German women in the process, and without a trace of self-awareness she prays fervently for her own safety. She also believes she has in her heart the best interests of the 'Gallant blacks' whose safety is almost as important to her as that of the white soldiers. Throughout the poem Betjeman reveals her as self-interested and self-deceiving. When she enumerates 'what our Nation stands for', she means the things that make her life a little better. The final emphasis on 'proper drains' sounds a note of bathos. The poem's setting in a church indicates that her social and ethical lapses result from her spiritual state. Her moral flaws are, in short, sins. And because she speaks for England's ruling class, it could be argued by extension that Betjeman believes social problems are a direct result of a nation's spiritual sickness. The poem's setting in Westminister Abbey, the epicentre of English Christianity, rather than in a small parish church, may not be incidental. The woman's narrow views are not rare or localized but are indicative of the moral and spiritual failure of the nation.

This poem may satirize certain of England's faithful as spiritually lazy and hypocritical, but it is satire born in a belief that the tenets of Christianity are true, however poorly applied by its adherents.

Hymn

The Church's Restoration
  In eighteen-eighty-three
Has left for contemplation
  Not what there used to be.
How well the ancient woodwork
  Looks round the Rect'ry hall,
Memorial of the good work
  Of him who plann'd it all.

He who took down the pew-ends
  And sold them anywhere
But kindly spared a few ends
  Work'd up into a chair.
O worthy persecution
  Of dust! O hue divine!
O cheerful substitution,
  Thou varnishéd pitch-pine!

Church furnishing! Church furnishing!
  Sing art and crafty praise!
He gave the brass for burnishing
  He gave the thick red baize,
He gave the new addition,
  Pull'd down the dull old aisle,
—To pave the sweet transition
  He gave th' encaustic tile.

Of marble brown and veinéd
   He did the pulpit make;
He order'd windows stainéd
   Light red and crimson lake.
Sing on, with hymns uproarious,
   Ye humble and aloof,
Look up! and oh, how glorious
   He has restored the roof!

Electric Light and Heating

Alternately the fogs and rains
Fill up the dim November lanes,
The church's year is nearly done
And waiting Advent not begun,
Our congregations shrink and shrink;
We sneeze so much we cannot think.
We blow our noses through the prayers,
And coughing takes us unawares;
We think of funerals and shrouds.
Our breath comes out in steamy clouds
Because the heating, we are told,
Will not be used *until it's cold.*
With aching limbs and throbbing head
We wish we were at home in bed.
    Oh! brave November congregation
Accept these lines of commendation;
You are the Church's prop and wall,
You keep it standing for us all!
    And now I'll turn to things more bright.
I'll talk about electric light.
Last year when Mr Sidney Groves
Said he'd no longer do the stoves
It gave the chance to Mrs Camps
To say she would not do the lamps,
And that gave everyone the chance
To cry, 'Well, let us have a dance!'
And so we did, we danced and danced
Until our funds were so advanced
That, helped by jumble sales and whist,
We felt that we could now insist
—So healthy was the cash position—
On calling in the electrician.

We called him in, and now, behold,
Our church is overlit and cold.
We have two hundred more to pay
Or go to gaol next Quarter Day.
    Despite the most impressive prices
Of our electrical devices,
And though the Bishop blessed the switches
Which now deface two ancient niches,
We do not like the electric light,
It's far too hard and bare and bright,
As for the heat, the bills are hot.
Unluckily the heating's not.
    They fell'd our elms to bring the wire,
They clamped their brackets on the spire
So that the church, one has to own,
Seems to be on the telephone.
Inside, they used our timbered roof,
Five centuries old and weather proof,
For part of their floodlighting scheme,
With surgical basins on each beam.
And if the bulbs in them should fuse
Or burst in fragments on the pews,
The longest ladder we possess
Would not reach up to mend the mess.
Talking of messes— you should see
The Electrician's artistry,
His Clapham-Junction-like creation
Of pipes and wires and insulation
Of meters, boxes, tubes, and all
Upon our ancient painted wall.
    If Sidney Groves and Mrs Camps
Had only done the stoves and lamps
These shameful things we would not see
Which rob our church of mystery.

The Friends of the Cathedral

At the end of our Cathedral
  Where people buy and sell
It says 'Friends of the Cathedral',
  And I'm sure they wish it well.

Perhaps they gave the bookstall
  Of modernistic oak,
And the chairs for the assistants
  And the ashtrays for a smoke.

Is it they who range the marigolds
  In pots of art design
About 'The Children's Corner',
  That very sacred shrine?

And do they hang the notices
  Off old crusader's toes?
And paint the cheeks of effigies
  That curious shade of rose?

Those things that look like wireless sets
  Suspended from each column,
Which bellow out the Litany
  Parsonically solemn—

Are these a present from the Friends?
  And if they are, how nice
That aided by their echo
  One can hear the service twice.

The hundred little bits of script
   Each framed in passe-partout
And nailed below the monuments,
   A clerical 'Who's Who'—

Are they as well the work of Friends?
   And do they also choose
The chantry chapel curtains
   In dainty tea-shop blues?

The Friends of the Cathedral—
   Are they friendly with the Dean?
And if they do things on their own
   What does their friendship mean?

Not Necessarily Leeds

I wish you could meet our delightful Archdeacon
There is not a thing he's unable to speak on.
And if what he says does not seem to you clear,
You will have to admit he's extremely sincere.

Yes, he is a man with his feet on the ground,
His financial arrangements are clever and sound.
I find as his Bishop I'm daily delighted
To think of the livings his skill has united.

Let me take for example St Peter the Least[1]
Which was staffed by a most irresponsible priest;
There are fewer less prejudiced persons than I
But the services there were impossibly High.

Its strange congregation was culled from afar,
And you know how eclectic such worshippers are.
The stipend was small but the site was worth more
Than any old church I have sold here before.

---

[1]   A church closed by the Bishop of London in 1953 and sold for £150,000.

St Barnabas, Oxford

How long was the peril, how breathless the day,
In topaz and beryl, the sun dies away,
His rays lying static at quarter to six
On polychromatical lacing of bricks.
Good Lord, as the angelus floats down the road,
Byzantine St Barnabas, be Thine Abode.

Where once the fritillaries hung in the grass
A baldachin pillar is guarding the Mass.
Farewell to blue meadows we loved not enough,
And elms in whose shadows were Glanville and Clough[1]
Not poets but clergymen hastened to meet
Thy redden'd remorselessness, Cardigan Street.

---

[1] John Glanvill (1664–1735) and Arthur Hugh Clough (1819–61) were poets and scholars at Oxford.

Exchange of Livings

The church was locked, so I went to the incumbent—
the incumbent enjoying a supine incumbency—
a tennis court, a summerhouse, deckchairs by the walnut tree
and only the hum of the bees in the rockery.
'May I have the keys of the church, your incumbency?'
'Yes, my dear sir, as a moderate churchman,
I am willing to exchange: light Sunday duty:
    nice district: pop 149: eight hundred per annum:
no extremes: A and M:[1] bicyclist essential:
      same income expected.'
'I think I'm the man that you want, your incumbency.
Here's my address when I'm not on my bicycle, poking
      about for recumbent stone effigies—
14, Mount Ephraim, Cheltenham, Glos:
Rector St George-in-the-Rolling Pins, Cripplegate:
non resident pop in the City of London:
eight fifty per annum (but verger an asset):
willing to exchange (no extremes) for incumbency,
similar income, but closer to residence.'

---

[1] *Hymns Ancient and Modern*: Church of England hymnal compiled by H.W. Baker.
Much used during the nineteenth and twentieth centuries, and deemed less high
church than *The English Hymnal*.

Blame the Vicar

When things go wrong it's rather tame
To find we are ourselves to blame,
It gets the trouble over quicker
To go and blame things on the Vicar.
The Vicar, after all, is paid
To keep us bright and undismayed.
The Vicar is more virtuous too
Than lay folks such as me and you.
He never swears, he never drinks,
He never *should* say what he thinks.
His collar is the wrong way round,
And that is why he's simply bound
To be the sort of person who
Has nothing very much to do
But take the blame for what goes wrong
And sing in tune at Evensong.
    For what's a Vicar really for
Except to cheer us up? What's more,
He shouldn't ever, ever tell
If there is such a place as Hell,
For if there is it's certain he
Will go to it as well as we.
The Vicar should be all pretence
And never, never give offence.
To preach on Sunday is his task
And lend his mower when we ask
And organize our village fêtes
And sing at Christmas with the waits
And in his car to give us lifts
And when we quarrel, heal the rifts.
To keep his family alive
He should industriously strive

In that enormous house he gets,
And he should always pay his debts,
For he has quite six pounds a week,
And when we're rude he should be meek
And always turn the other cheek.
He should be neat and nicely dressed
With polished shoes and trousers pressed,
For we look up to him as higher
Than anyone, except the Squire.

    Dear People, who have read so far,
I know how really kind you are,
I hope that you are always seeing
Your Vicar as a human being,
Making allowances when he
Does things with which you don't agree.
But there are lots of people who
Are not so kind to him as you.
So in conclusion you shall hear
About a parish somewhere near,
Perhaps your own or maybe not,
And of the Vicars that it got.
    One parson came and people said,
'Alas! Our former Vicar's dead!
And this new man is far more "Low"
Than dear old Reverend so-and-so,
And far too earnest in his preaching,
We do not really like his teaching,
He seems to think we're simply fools
Who've never been to Sunday Schools.'
That Vicar left, and by and by
A new one came, 'He's much too "High",'
The people said, 'too like a saint,
His incense makes our Mavis faint.'

So now he's left and they're alone
Without a Vicar of their own.
The living's been amalgamated
With one next door they've always hated.

Dear readers, from this rhyme take warning,
And if you heard the bell this morning
Your Vicar went to pray for you,
A task the Prayer Book bids him do.
'Highness' or 'Lowness' do not matter,
You are the Church and must not scatter,
Cling to the Sacraments and pray
And God be with you every day.

The Parochial Church Council

Last week a friend inquired of me,
'Oh, should I join our P.C.C.?'
I answered, rather priggishly,
'If you communicate, you can,
And want to help your clergyman.
Parochial Church Councils are
From Parish Councils different far.'
I said, 'And District Councils too
Have very different things to do,
For District Councils raise the rates
And have political debates.
If one side says "Preserve the Town",
The other side says "Pull it down!"
And Parish Councils try to make
The District Council keep awake
To local practical affairs—
Like village bus-shelter repairs.
Parish and Parliament and Queen,
A mighty structure thus is seen—
Endless committees in between.
And I suppose that it occurr'd
To someone as not quite absurd
To make our Church of England be
A similar democracy.
The Church Assembly's near the top,
Where people talk until they drop;
Next come Diocesan Committees,
Like Mayor and Aldermen in cities.
The equivalent to R.D.C.'s
Are ruri-decanal jamborees,
And at the root of all the tree
We find the homely P.C.C.

For P.C.C.'s were really made
To give your local vicar aid,
And I have always understood
That most of them are very good—
Where lay folk do what jobs they can
To help their church and clergyman.
But in small villages I've known
Of ones that make the vicar groan
And wish he could be left alone.
So just you come along with me
To a really wicked P.C.C.

'Tis evening in the village school,
And perched upon an infant's stool
The village postmistress is sitting
Glancing at us above her knitting.
Like schoolchildren—but do not laugh—
Farmers in desks too small by half;
Prim ladies, brooding for a storm
Are ranged like infants, on a form.
We read the text that hangs above
In coloured letters "GOD is LOVE".
The Vicar takes the teacher's chair,
A dreadful tenseness fills the air.
"We will begin," he says, "with prayer."
We do. It doesn't make things better.
The Vicar reads the Bishop's letter—
"Diocesan this and quota that"—
He might be talking through his hat;
It is not what they've come about.
And now the devil's jumping out
For next we have the church accounts,
And as they're read, the tension mounts.
This Vicar has been forced to be
The Treasurer of his P.C.C.,

As no one else will volunteer
To do the hard work needed here.
"Well, Vicar, do I understand
Last year we had six pounds in hand?"
Says Farmer Pinch who's rich and round
And lord of ninety thousand pound,
"And this year you are three pound ten
In debt—and in the red again.
Now, Vicar, that is not the way
To make a parson's business pay.
You're losing cash. It's got to stop
Or you will have to shut up shop."
The tactless Vicar answers, "Sir,
Upon the church you cast a slur:
Church is not Trade"; "Then time it were,"
Says Farmer Pinch. And now Miss Right
Who has been spoiling for a fight—
Miss Right who thinks she's very Low
And cannot bring herself to go
To services where people kneel,
Miss Right who always makes you feel
You're in the wrong, and sulks at home
And says the Vicar's paid by Rome—
Cries "If the Vicar and his pals
Spent less on Popish fal-de-lals
Like altar candles and such frills
Perhaps we then could pay our bills."
The fight grows furious and thicker,
And what was meant to help the Vicar—
This democratic P.C.C.—
Seems just the opposite to me.
The meeting soon is charged with hate,
And turns the Devil's advocate:
Its members do not come to church.
Admittedly you'd have to search

A lot of villages to find
A P.C.C. that's so unkind,
But everywhere, just now and then,
The Devil tempts the best of men;
So if you join your P.C.C.
Be calm and full of charity.'

Diary of a Church Mouse

Here among long-discarded cassocks,
Damp stools, and half-split open hassocks,
Here where the Vicar never looks
I nibble through old service books.
Lean and alone I spend my days
Behind this Church of England baize.
I share my dark forgotten room
With two oil-lamps and half a broom.
The cleaner never bothers me,
So here I eat my frugal tea.
My bread is sawdust mixed with straw;
My jam is polish for the floor.

    Christmas and Easter may be feasts
For congregations and for priests,
And so may Whitsun. All the same,
They do not fill my meagre frame.
For me the only feast at all
Is Autumn's Harvest Festival,
When I can satisfy my want
With ears of corn around the font.
I climb the eagle's brazen head
To burrow through a loaf of bread.
I scramble up the pulpit stair
And gnaw the marrows hanging there.

    It is enjoyable to taste
These items ere they go to waste,
But how annoying when one finds
That other mice with pagan minds
Come into church my food to share
Who have no proper business there.
Two field mice who have no desire
To be baptized, invade the choir.

A large and most unfriendly rat
Comes in to see what we are at.
He says he thinks there is no God
And yet he comes ... it's rather odd.
This year he stole a sheaf of wheat
(It screened our special preacher's seat),
And prosperous mice from fields away
Come in to hear the organ play,
And under cover of its notes
Ate through the altar's sheaf of oats.
A Low Church mouse, who thinks that I
Am too papistical, and High,
Yet somehow doesn't think it wrong
To munch through Harvest Evensong,
While I, who starve the whole year through,
Must share my food with rodents who
Except at this time of the year
Not once inside the church appear.
    Within the human world I know
Such goings-on could not be so,
For human beings only do
What their religion tells them to.
They read the Bible every day
And always, night and morning, pray,
And just like me, the good church mouse,
Worship each week in God's own house,
    But all the same it's strange to me
How very full the church can be
With people I don't see at all
Except at Harvest Festival.

Guilt

The clock is frozen in the tower,
    The thickening fog with sooty smell
Has blanketed the motor power
    Which turns the London streets to hell;
And footsteps with their lonely sound
Intensify the silence round.

I haven't hope. I haven't faith.
    I live two lives and sometimes three.
The lives I live make life a death
    For those who have to live with me.
Knowing the virtues that I lack,
I pat myself upon the back.

With breastplate of self-righteousness
    And shoes of smugness on my feet,
Before the urge in me grows less
    I hurry off to make retreat.
For somewhere, somewhere, burns a light
To lead me out into the night.

It glitters icy, thin and plain,
    And leads me down to Waterloo—
Into a warm electric train
    Which travels sorry Surrey through
Where, crystal-hung, the clumps of pine
Stand deadly still beside the line.

Bristol and Clifton[1]

'Yes, I was only sidesman here when last
You came to Evening Communion.
But now I have retired from the bank
I have more leisure time for church finance.
We moved into a somewhat larger house
Than when you knew us in Manilla Road.
This is the window to my lady wife.
You cannot see it now, but in the day
The greens and golds are truly wonderful.'

'How very sad. I do not mean about
The window, but I mean about the death
Of Mrs. Battlecock. When did she die?'

'Two years ago when we had just moved in
To Pembroke Road. I rather fear the stairs
And basement kitchen were too much for her—
Not that, of course, she did the servants' work—
But supervising servants all the day
Meant quite a lot of climbing up and down.'

'How very sad. Poor Mrs. Battlecock.'
'"The glory that men do lives after them,"
And so I gave this window in her name.
It's executed by a Bristol firm;

---

[1] The church described here is said by Bevis Hillier to be Emmanuel Church, Clifton
(*John Betjeman: New Fame, New Love*, pp. 281–2). Declared redundant in 1974,
Emmanuel Church was demolished to build flats for the elderly. Only the tower
remains and is incorporated into the new structure.

This poem cleverly echoes Browning's 'My Last Duchess'.

The lady artist who designed it, made
The figure of the lady on the left
Something like Mrs. Battlecock.'
'How nice.'

       'Yes, was it not? We had
A stained glass window on the stairs at home,
In Pembroke Road. But not so good as this.
This window is the glory of the church
At least I think so—and the unstained oak
Looks very chaste beneath it. When I gave
The oak, that brass inscription on your right
Commemorates the fact, the Dorcas Club
Made these blue kneelers, though we do not kneel:
We leave that to the Roman Catholics.'
'How very nice, indeed. How very nice.'

'Seeing I have some knowledge of finance
Our kind Parochial Church Council made
Me People's Warden, and I'm glad to say
That our collections are still keeping up.
The chancel has been flood-lit, and the stove
Which used to heat the church was obsolete.
So now we've had some radiators fixed
Along the walls and eastward of the aisles;
This last I thought of lest at any time
A Ritualist should be inducted here
And want to put up altars. He would find
The radiators inconvenient.
Our only ritual here is with the Plate;
I think we make it dignified enough.
I take it up myself, and afterwards,
Count the Collection on the vestry safe.'

'Forgive me, aren't we talking rather loud?
I think I see a woman praying there.'
'Praying? The service is all over now
And here's the verger waiting to turn out
The lights and lock the church up. She cannot
Be Loyal Church of England. Well, goodbye.
Time flies. I must be going. Come again.
There are some pleasant people living here.
I know the Inskips very well indeed.'

St Mary Magdalen, Old Fish Street Hill

On winter evenings I walk alone in the City
    When cobbles glisten with wet and it's foggy and still;
I am Rector's warden here. But more's the pity
    We haven't the Charity children now to fill
Our old west gallery front. Some new committee
    Has done away with them all. I beg your pardon,
    I omitted to tell you where I am Rector's warden—
At St Mary Magdalen's church, Old Fish Street Hill.[1]

Unfortunately, the London Conflagration
    Of sixteen sixty-six was a moment when
The Roman style in general estimation
    Was held so high that our church was rebuilt by Wren.
It is just a box with a fanciful plaster ceiling
Devoid of a vestige of genuine Christian feeling,
    And our congregation is seldom more than ten.

---

[1] Although rebuilt by Christopher Wren after the Great Fire of 1666, this church was lost to another fire in 1886 and never rebuilt.

In Westminster Abbey

Let me take this other glove off
　　As the *vox humana* swells,
And the beauteous fields of Eden
　　Bask beneath the Abbey bells.
Here, where England's statesmen lie,
Listen to a lady's cry.

Gracious Lord, oh bomb the Germans.
　　Spare their women for Thy Sake,
And if that is not too easy
　　We will pardon Thy Mistake.
But, gracious Lord, whate'er shall be,
Don't let anyone bomb me.

Keep our Empire undismembered
　　Guide our Forces by Thy Hand,
Gallant blacks from far Jamaica,
　　Honduras and Togoland;
Protect them Lord in all their fights,
And, even more, protect the whites.

Think of what our Nation stands for,
　　Books from Boots' and country lanes,
Free speech, free passes, class distinction,
　　Democracy and proper drains.
Lord, put beneath Thy special care
One-eighty-nine Cadogan Square.

Although dear Lord I am a sinner,
    I have done no major crime;
Now I'll come to Evening Service
    Whensoever I have the time.
So, Lord, reserve for me a crown,
And do not let my shares go down.

I will labour for Thy Kingdom,
    Help our lads to win the war,
Send white feathers to the cowards
    Join the Women's Army Corps,
Then wash the Steps around Thy Throne
In the Eternal Safety Zone.

Now I feel a little better,
    What a treat to hear Thy Word,
Where the bones of leading statesmen,
    Have so often been interr'd.
And now, dear Lord, I cannot wait
Because I have a luncheon date.

6

The Decline of England

6 The Decline of England

It may seem unusual to include among Betjeman's religious verse a group of poems lamenting the enervation of English culture and the despoliation of the English landscape. Many of these poems are harsh attacks on what Betjeman perceived to be a desecration of both city and country, from litter to pylons to concrete office blocks, and his anger and bitterness, though sometimes disguised by an ironic serenity, is meant to reflect the increasing ugliness in his beloved nation. There is a long tradition of semi-mythological English landscape poetry that blends pastoral yearning for an imagined past with a sense that such cultural loss has a moral or spiritual dimension. This diverse context includes John of Gaunt's paean to England in *Richard II* ('This other Eden, demi-paradise') and Blake's 'Jerusalem' ('And was the holy Lamb of God / On England's pleasant pastures seen?'), as well as popular songs such as Ivor Novello's 'The Land of Might-Have-Been' ('Somewhere there's another land, / Different from this world below'), all of which evoke an imaginary but spiritual England just beyond our grasp. If we consider Betjeman's poems on a declining England within this poetic context it becomes apparent that his views on progress and preservation are rooted in his religious beliefs. To Betjeman, England was once Edenic but has been recklessly ruined by modern progress. In updating the image of dark Satanic mills with one of power stations, Betjeman sustains Blake's notion that progress is a euphemism for social action that masks the sinful nature of humanity. The result is a fallen world; England is only a memory, a land that might have been.

Reading Betjeman's verse in this light allows us to see that he has infused with spirituality his opinions of architectural and landscape preservation, of urban and pastoral blight, and of the forsaken customs and symbols of England.

The first three of these poems relate the beauty of the English landscape to the innocence of childhood and by extension the desecration of that landscape to a loss of innocence. 'Lines Written to Martyn Skinner' praises the poet's friend for his escape from the urban wasteland of modern Oxford into a bucolic England of boyhood dreams. In Ealing Skinner will find a euphonic paradise of church bells and birds and milkmen, and will leave behind the grating urban cacophony of power plants, motorbikes and lorries. Here Betjeman connects the purity and innocence of childhood with an unspoiled landscape, while in 'Hertfordshire' he connects a childhood mortification with the devastation of natural beauty. Though predominantly a meditation on a memory of a humiliating hunting trip with his father, 'Hertfordshire' concludes with a disaster much greater than the poet's shame at mishandling his gun and disappointing his father, the rape of the pastoral countryside by the emblems of progress: electric wires, concrete poles and suburban sprawl. 'Delectable Duchy' observes a similar transformation in Cornwall. The natural emptiness of its scenic coastline has been corrupted by humanity and its detritus: cellophane wrappers, abandoned toys, caravans, portable toilets and, perhaps the most offensive litter of all, villas that 'hog' an ocean view once open to all. Like the first two poems, this one also equates a pristine landscape with the carefree days of childhood; Betjeman imagines a time when Cornwall's shores were 'unpeopled', but now the Duchy is 'gone beyond recall'. Imbuing these poems with a spiritual dimension, Betjeman suggests a link between an unmolested countryside and prelapsarian innocence, which further implies that the ongoing violation of the English landscape has resulted from a moral fall.

The next four poems all employ varying degrees of irony to castigate this new England: an England of litter, pollution and blight. Blindly praising the modern face of England, the speakers in these poems are either apathetic to or oblivious of the horrors besetting counties, farms, villages and the entire nation. 'Cheshire' describes an entire county corrupted by transgression of aesthetic principles. Everywhere is an architectural impropriety plastered onto nature, from rooflines in the Dutch style to faux medieval golfing clubs, an aesthetic jumble worsened by a mish-mash of transportation routes and a horizon criss-crossed by wires. Betjeman's point is to create a mental hodge-podge that not only confuses but also offends against both taste and morals. As its title suggests, 'Harvest Hymn' appropriates an ecclesial probity in its assault on agrarian England. Here Betjeman asks us to recall a traditional farming life, now essentially gone for ever. Small, bucolic farms having been swallowed up by monstrous cooperatives, the new farm is a nightmare of pesticides, overproduction and materialism. Except when spraying poisons and burning ancient hedgerows, farmers are entirely cut off from their land and their history. Without thought for the future, their mantra is 'The earth is ours today.' To Betjeman the natural English landscape also includes man-made features, so long as they are ancient. These are especially apparent in the village and include the parish church, public footpaths, thatched-roof cottages and the pub. 'The Dear Old Village' is Betjeman's ironic celebration of the English village transformed, updated and improved by progress. Much of the poem excoriates a greedy and hypocritical local farmer who sells his 'useless' land for the construction of council houses. Residents suffer in ugly and unsafe houses while village children are sent by bus to a distant, modern school whose curriculum teaches them to scorn their past. On Sundays the church has little reason to open its doors to its three feckless parishioners, while the village youth ride off to the cinema on motorbikes that drown the echoing church bells. 'Inexpensive

Progress' makes brilliant use of irony to expose the cheapness of modern progress and the vast expense of its devastation nationwide. 'Progress' includes offences major and minor: power stations and nylon stockings are among Betjeman's targets, along with electrical pylons, motorways, landing-strips and plate-glass windows. In addition to green spaces, other traditional features of the English landscape lost to progress include country lanes, hedgerows and inn signs. Throughout the poem the denunciation of modernity is rendered in moral and religious terms: to Betjeman this is a soulless age; the effects of progress are obscene; and the result of it all is death. The degree of Betjeman's wrath can be measured in his suggestion that progress is a kind of monstrous intestinal effluvium, yet the religious fervour of the poem turns his anger from bitterness into righteousness.

An entire nation is clearly to blame for these execrations against the traditional English landscape, but the locus of Betjeman's rage is the civil servant with a passion for expunging the past and a loathing for the preservationist's instinct. 'The Planster's Vision' captures remarkably the sort of voice never before heard in a sonnet. This is the voice of bureaucracy, a town planner anxious to erase the symbols of English history and replant the landscape with a Maoist vision of collective banality. Betjeman fulminates against a dystopic future in which church bells are silenced by loudspeakers indoctrinating the masses until they have become brainwashed drones. 'The Town Clerk's Views' is a lengthier elaboration of this same nightmare, leisurely unfolding in a plan 'to turn our country into hell'. The vision begins with pulling down traditional cottages in favour of massive flats of concrete, glass and steel. It then encompasses the restructuring of county borders wherein a disregard for history means that some counties no longer have any justification for an independent existence; their names too are out of date and ought to be reconfigured with terminology redolent of London's postal codes. Blandness and uniformity are the operative principles in the town clerk's vision of England. In academic centres, Oxford, having carelessly thrown up concrete blocks everywhere, is on the right path, but poor Cambridge, clinging still to its useless chapels, halls and backs, is out of touch with the march of progress. As religion has no place in this utopia, cathedrals can now be transformed into cultural centres, and sermons on the effects of sin will be supplanted with lectures of a civil or sociological nature. The crowning glory of the town planner's vision for a modern England is the expunging of religion. God has no place in this hellish future, and the horror for Betjeman is that English tradition will have arrived at its demise.

The state's displacement and appropriation of the Church not only debilitates the village but also hastens the rise of an alien and fatuous modern city. 'Huxley Hall' suggests a brave new world indeed, a dystopian vision of an England where every town has become Welwyn or Milton Keynes. Despite the efforts of modern planners to undermine the influence of religion, Betjeman instinctively dwells on the evidence that humans are by nature sinful and have fallen as a result. The behaviour of 'innocent' children at play as well as of bureaucratic hypocrites bolsters his belief. The state has made a futile effort to perfect human existence, and it maintains the pleasant fiction of evolutionary progress for humanity. However, it has denied him pleasures by regulating his diet, and he has sunk into depression caused by the state's every effort to improve society. The state, having presumed to usurp God as redeemer of humanity, has failed and fallen, creating instead a 'bright, hygienic hell'. In contrast with the illusory purity and piety of 'Huxley Hall' is the brazen horror and doom of 'Chelsea 1977'. Here Betjeman describes the beauty of a city sunset despoiled by piles of excrement, building materials, sewage pipes and so forth. Betjeman transforms this urban wasteland into a literal hell as Satan lurks just beneath the streets, fanning his flames to heighten the eternal torment for those who have blighted England.

'Slough' also denies the modern city the comfortable fiction of cleanliness. In this poem written just before the war, Betjeman saw the town of Slough as not merely an excrescence of arresting ugliness and mundanity but a moral morass of modernism that rendered it unfit for human occupation. 'Slough' is one of Betjeman's most famous poems and perhaps his harshest indictment of humanity: he rebukes us for our materialism, our insensitivity to our environment, our moral and sexual corruption and our indolent preference for the benefits of modern technology at the expense of traditional culture. The desecration of culture and landscape being complete and irreversible, 'Slough' suggests that annihilation is to be desired. Only complete decimation can purge and purify the England represented by Slough and prepare it for a reawakening. Despite the apparent viciousness of Betjeman's apostrophic petition, 'Come, friendly bombs, and fall on Slough', the poet is motivated by righteous indignation. The poem feels like a jeremiad yet ends with a hopeful image in its depiction of the post-apocalyptic aftermath. The bombs will make the place more attractive and fit for habitation. The bombs will expunge the evils of Slough in order to restore to it a traditional, agrarian England. The bombs may be coming, but after them will come the plough and the cabbages. As the earth renews it 'exhales', as if it has been holding its breath all this while against the stench of modern Slough. While this bucolic vision is undoubtedly a mere fantasy, a 'land of might have been', the idea behind it is not. What Betjeman yearns for is a restoration of religious proportions.

Lines written to Martyn Skinner[1] before his Departure from Oxfordshire in Search of Quiet – 1961

Return, return to Ealing,
    Worn poet of the farm!
Regain your boyhood feeling
    Of uninvaded calm!
For there the leafy avenues
    Of lime and chestnut mix'd
Do widely wind, by art designed,
    The costly houses 'twixt.

No early morning tractors
    The thrush and blackbird drown,
No nuclear reactors
    Bulge huge below the down,
No youth upon his motor-bike
    His lust for power fulfils,
With dentist's drill intent to kill
    The silence of the hills.

In Ealing on a Sunday
    Bell-haunted quiet falls,
In Ealing on a Monday
    'Milk-o!' the milkman calls;
No lorries grind in bottom gear
    Up steep and narrow lanes,
Nor constant here offend the ear
    Low-flying aeroplanes.

---

[1] Writer and friend of Betjeman's (1906–94).

Return, return to Ealing,
  Worn poet of the farm!
Regain your boyhood feeling
  Of uninvaded calm!
Where smoothly glides the bicycle
  And softly flows the Brent
And a gentle gale from Perivale
  Sends up the hayfield scent.

Hertfordshire

I had forgotten Hertfordshire,
    The large unwelcome fields of roots
Where with my knickerbockered sire
    I trudged in syndicated shoots;

And that unlucky day when I
    Fired by mistake into the ground
Under a Lionel Edwards[1] sky
    And felt disapprobation round.

The slow drive home by motor-car,
    A heavy Rover Landaulette,
Through Welwyn, Hatfield, Potters Bar,
    Tweed and cigar smoke, gloom and wet:

'How many times must I explain
    The way a boy should hold a gun?'
I recollect my father's pain
    At such a milksop for a son.

And now I see these fields once more
    Clothed, thank the Lord, in summer green,
Pale corn waves rippling to a shore
    The shadowy cliffs of elm between,

Colour-washed cottages reed-thatched
    And weather-boarded water mills,
Flint churches, brick and plaster patched,
    On mildly undistinguished hills—

[1] Watercolourist (1878–1966) noted for his hunting scenes.

They still are there. But now the shire
    Suffers a devastating change,
Its gentle landscape strung with wire,
    Old places looking ill and strange.

One can't be sure where London ends,
    New towns have filled the fields of root
Where father and his business friends
    Drove in the Landaulette to shoot;

Tall concrete standards line the lane,
    Brick boxes glitter in the sun:
Far more would these have caused him pain
    Than my mishandling of a gun.

Delectable Duchy

Where yonder villa hogs the sea
Was open cliff to you and me.
The many-coloured cara's fill
The salty marsh to Shilla Mill.[1]
And, foreground to the hanging wood,
Are toilets where the castle stood.
The mint and meadowsweet would scent
The brambly lane by which we went;
Now, as we near the ocean roar,
A smell of deep-fry haunts the shore.
In pools beyond the reach of tides
The Senior Service carton glides,
And on the sand the surf-line lisps
With wrappings of potato crisps.
The breakers bring with merry noise
Tribute of broken plastic toys
And lichened spears of blackthorn glitter
With harvest of the August litter.

Here in the late October light
See Cornwall, a pathetic sight,
Raddled and put upon and tired
And looking somewhat over-hired,
Remembering in the autumn air
The years when she was young and fair—
Those golden and unpeopled bays,
The shadowy cliffs and sheep-worn ways,
The white unpopulated surf,
The thyme- and mushroom-scented turf,

---

[1]   A medieval windmill near Polzeath, Cornwall.

The slate-hung farms, the oil-lit chapels,
Thin elms and lemon-coloured apples—
Going and gone beyond recall
Now she is free for 'One and All.'[1]

One day a tidal wave will break
Before the breakfasters awake
And sweep the cara's out to sea,
The oil, the tar, and you and me,
And leave in windy criss-cross motion
A waste of undulating ocean
With, jutting out, a second Scilly,
The isles of Roughtor and Brown Willy.

[1] Cornwall's official motto.

Cheshire

Infirmaries by Aston Webb[1]
    On ev'ry hill surmount the pines;
From two miles off you still can see
    Their terracotta Dutch designs
And metalled roads bisect canals,
    And both are crossed by railway lines.

And here a copse of Douglas firs
    Protects the merchant on the links;
The timbered club-house is not yet
    As mediaeval as he thinks;
For miles around the villas rise
    In hard interminable pinks.

Oh spin with me on pylon wires
    You Chester, Northwich, Knutsford chaps!
Look down on muddy empty fields
    And empty sheds and foot-worn gaps,
And pipes, and recreation grounds,
    And then content yourselves with maps.

---

[1] Victorian architect (1849–1930), who on occasion used the pseudonym 'Terracotta'. His most famous designs are the Admiralty Arch and the entrance facade of Buckingham Palace. In an essay in *Country Life*, Betjeman referred to Webb's work as 'frankly awkward'.

Harvest Hymn[1]

We spray the fields and scatter
    The poison on the ground
So that no wicked wild flowers
    Upon our farm be found.
We like whatever helps us
    To line our purse with pence;
The twenty-four-hour broiler-house
    And neat electric fence.

All concrete sheds around us
    And Jaguars in the yard,
The telly lounge and deep-freeze
    Are ours from working hard.

We fire the fields for harvest,
    The hedges swell the flame,
The oak trees and the cottages
    From which our fathers came.
We give no compensation,
    The earth is ours today,
And if we lose on arable,
    Then bungalows will pay.

All concrete sheds . . . etc.

---

[1] Parody of the well-known harvest hymn 'We plough the fields and scatter'.

The Dear Old Village

The dear old village! *Lin-lan-lone* the bells
(Which should be six) ring over hills and dells,
But since the row about the ringers' tea
It's *lin-lan-lone*. They're only ringing three.
The elm leaves patter like a summer shower
As *lin-lan-lone* pours through them from the tower.
From that embattled, lichen-crusted fane
Which scoops the sun into each western pane,
The bells ring over hills and dells in vain.
For we are free today. No need to praise
The Unseen Author of our nights and days;
No need to hymn the rich uncurling spring
For DYKES is nowhere half so good as BING.[1]
Nature is out of date and GOD is too;
Think what atomic energy can do!

 Farmers have wired the public rights-of-way
Should any wish to walk to church to pray.
Along the village street the sunset strikes
On young men turning up their motor-bikes,
And country girls with lips and nails vermilion
Wait, nylon-legged, to straddle on the pillion.
Off to the roadhouse and the Tudor Bar
And then the Sunday-opened cinema.
While to the church's iron-studded door
Go two old ladies and a child of four.

 This is the age of progress. Let us meet
The new progressives of the village street.
Hear not the water lapsing down the rills,
Lift not your eyes to the surrounding hills,

---

[1] Bing Crosby (1903–77) was a popular American singer. John Bacchus Dykes (1823–76) composed more than 300 hymn tunes.

While spring recalls the miracle of birth
Let us, for heaven's sake, keep down to earth.
   See that square house, late Georgian and smart,
Two fields away it proudly stands apart,
Dutch barn and concrete cow-sheds have replaced
The old thatched roofs which once the yard disgraced.
Here wallows Farmer WHISTLE[1] in his riches,
His ample stomach heaved above his breeches.
You'd never think that in such honest beef
Lurk'd an adulterous braggart, liar and thief.
His wife brought with her thirty-thousand down:
He keeps his doxy in the nearest town.
No man more anxious on the R.D.C.
For better rural cottages than he,
Especially when he had some land to sell
Which, as a site, would suit the Council well.
So three times what he gave for it he got,
For one undrainable and useless plot
Where now the hideous Council houses stand.
Unworked on and unworkable their land,
The wind blows under each unseason'd door,
The floods pour over every kitchen floor,
And country wit, which likes to laugh at sin,
Christens the Council houses 'Whistle's Win'.
Woe to some lesser farmer who may try
To call his bluff or to expose his lie.
Remorseless as a shark in London's City,
He gets at them through the War Ag. Committee.
   He takes no part in village life beyond
Throwing his refuse in a neighbour's pond
And closing footpaths, not repairing walls,
Leaving a cottage till at last it falls.
People protest. A law-suit then begins,
But as he's on the Bench, he always wins.

---

[1] A parodic portrait of John Wheeler, the Betjemans' landlord in Uffington.

Behind rank elders, shadowing a pool,
And near the Church, behold the Village School,
Its gable rising out of ivy thick
Shows 'Eighteen-Sixty' worked in coloured brick.
By nineteen-forty-seven, hurrah! hooray
This institution has outlived its day.
In the bad times of old feudality
The villagers were ruled by masters three—
Squire, parson, schoolmaster. Of these, the last
Knew best the village present and its past.
Now, I am glad to say, the man is dead,
The children have a motor-bus instead,
And in a town eleven miles away
We train them to be 'Citizens of Today'.
And many a cultivated hour they pass
In a fine school with walls of vita-glass.
Civics, eurhythmics, economics, Marx,
How-to-respect-wild-life-in-National-Parks;
Plastics, gymnastics—thus they learn to scorn
The old thatch'd cottages where they were born.
The girls, ambitious to begin their lives
Serving in WOOLWORTH'S, rather than as wives;
The boys, who cannot yet escape the land,
At driving tractors lend a clumsy hand.
An eight-hour day for all, and more than three
Of these are occupied in making tea
And talking over what we all agree—
Though 'Music while you work' is now our wont,
It's not so nice as 'Music while you don't.'
Squire, parson, schoolmaster turn in their graves.
And *let* them turn. We are no longer slaves.

So much for youth. I fear we older folk
Must be dash'd off with a more hurried stroke.
Old Mrs. SPEAK has cut, for fifteen years,
Her husband's widowed sister Mrs. SHEARS,

Though how she's managed it, I cannot say,
Sharing a cottage with her night and day.
What caused the quarrel fifteen years ago
And how BERT SPEAK gets on, I do not know,
There the three live in that old dwelling quaint
Which water-colourists delight to paint.
Of the large brood round Mrs. COKER'S door,
Coker has definitely fathered four
And two are Farmer Whistle's: two they say
Have coloured fathers in the U.S.A.
I learn'd all this and more from Mrs. FREE,
Pride of the Women's Institute is she,
Says 'Sir' or 'Madam' to you, knows her station
And how to make a quiet insinuation.
The unrespectable must well know why
They fear her lantern jaw and leaden eye.
      There is no space to tell about the chaps—
Which pinch, which don't, which beat their wives with
            straps.

Go to the Inn on any Friday night
And listen to them while they're getting tight
At the expense of him who stands them drinks,
The Mass-Observer[1] with the Hillman Minx.[2]
(Unwitting he of all the knowing winks)
The more he circulates the bitter ales
The longer and the taller grow the tales.
'Ah! this is England,' thinks he, 'rich and pure
As tilth and loam and wains and horse-manure,
Slow—yes. But sociologically sound.'
'Landlord!' he cries, 'the same again all round!'

---

[1] 'Mass Observation' is a social research organization started in 1937 using both paid and voluntary writers to observe, study and record their impressions of everyday behaviour in the UK, especially in public settings such as in council meetings or in pubs. The project continued until the early 1950s; revived in 1981, it continues to this day.
[2] British car of the 1950s: small and practical.

Inexpensive Progress

Encase your legs in nylons,
Bestride your hills with pylons
   O age without a soul;
Away with gentle willows
And all the elmy billows
   That through your valleys roll.

Let's say goodbye to hedges
And roads with grassy edges
   And winding country lanes;
Let all things travel faster
Where motor-car is master
   Till only Speed remains.

Destroy the ancient inn-signs
But strew the roads with tin signs
   'Keep Left', 'M4', 'Keep Out!'
Command, instruction, warning,
Repetitive adorning
   The rockeried roundabout;

For every raw obscenity
Must have its small 'amenity,'
   Its patch of shaven green,
And hoardings look a wonder
In banks of floribunda
   With floodlights in between.

Leave no old village standing
Which could provide a landing
   For aeroplanes to roar,

But spare such cheap defacements
As huts with shattered casements
   Unlived-in since the war.

Let no provincial High Street
Which might be your or my street
   Look as it used to do,
But let the chain stores place here
Their miles of black glass facia
   And traffic thunder through.

And if there is some scenery,
Some unpretentious greenery,
   Surviving anywhere,
It does not need protecting
For soon we'll be erecting
   A Power Station there.

When all our roads are lighted
By concrete monsters sited
   Like gallows overhead,
Bathed in the yellow vomit
Each monster belches from it,
   We'll know that we are dead.

The Planster's[1] Vision

Cut down that timber! Bells, too many and strong,
    Pouring their music through the branches bare,
    From moon-white church-towers down the windy air
Have pealed the centuries out with Evensong.
Remove those cottages, a huddled throng!
    Too many babies have been born in there,
    Too many coffins, bumping down the stair,
Carried the old their garden paths along.

I have a Vision of The Future, chum,
    The workers' flats in fields of soya beans
    Tower up like silver pencils, score on score:
And Surging Millions hear the Challenge come
    From microphones in communal canteens
    'No Right! No Wrong! All's perfect, evermore.'

---

[1] A projector or schemer of urban development or reconstruction, used with pejorative connotations.

The Town Clerk's Views

'Yes, the Town Clerk will see you.' In I went.
He was, like all Town Clerks, from north of Trent;
A man with bye-laws busy in his head
Whose Mayor and Council followed where he led.
His most capacious brain will make us cower,
His only weakness is a lust for power—
And that is not a weakness, people think,
When unaccompanied by bribes or drink.
So let us hear this cool careerist tell
His plans to turn our country into hell.
'I cannot say how shock'd I am to see
The *variations* in our scenery.
Just take for instance, at a casual glance,
Our muddled coastline opposite to France:
Dickensian houses by the Channel tides
With old hipp'd roofs and weather-boarded sides.
I blush to think one corner of our isle
Lacks concrete villas in the modern style.
Straight lines of hops in pale brown earth of Kent,
Yeomen's square houses once, no doubt, content
With willow-bordered horse-pond, oast-house, shed,
Wide orchard, garden walls of browny-red—
All useless now, but what fine sites they'ld be
For workers' flats and some light industry.
Those lumpy church towers, unadorned with spires,
And wavy roofs that burn like smouldering fires
In sharp spring sunlight over ashen flint
Are out of date as some old aquatint.
Then glance below the line of Sussex downs
To stucco terraces of seaside towns
Turn'd into flats and residential clubs
Above the wind-slashed Corporation shrubs.

Such Georgian relics should by now, I feel,
Be all rebuilt in glass and polished steel.
Bournemouth is looking up. I'm glad to say
That modernistic there has come to stay.
I walk the asphalt paths of Branksome Chine
In resin-scented air like strong Greek wine
And dream of cliffs of flats along those heights,
Floodlit at night with green electric lights.
But as for Dorset's flint and Purbeck stone,
Its old thatched farms in dips of down alone—
It should be merged with Hants and made to be
A self-contained and plann'd community.
Like Flint and Rutland, it is much too small
And has no reason to exist at all.
Of Devon one can hardly say the same,
But "South-West Area One" 's a better name
For those red sandstone cliffs that stain the sea
By mid-Victoria's Italy—Torquay.
But "South-West Area Two" could well include
The whole of Cornwall from Land's End to Bude.
Need I retrace my steps through other shires?
Pinnacled Somerset? Northampton's spires?
Burford's broad High Street is descending still
Stone-roofed and golden-walled her elmy hill
To meet the river Windrush. What a shame
Her houses are not brick and all the same.
Oxford is growing up to date at last.
Cambridge, I fear, is living in the past.
She needs more factories, not useless things
Like that great chapel which they keep at King's.
As for remote East Anglia, he who searches
Finds only thatch and vast, redundant churches.
But that's the dark side. I can safely say
A beauteous England's really on the way.

Already our hotels are pretty good
For those who're fond of *very simple food*—
Cod and two veg., free pepper, salt and mustard,
Followed by nice hard plums and lumpy custard,
A pint of bitter beer for one-and-four,
Then coffee in the lounge a shilling more.
In a few years this country will be looking
As uniform and tasty as its cooking.
Hamlets which fail to pass the planners' test
Will be demolished. We'll rebuild the rest
To look like Welwyn mixed with Middle West.
All fields we'll turn to sports grounds, lit at night
From concrete standards by fluorescent light:
And over all the land, instead of trees,
Clean poles and wire will whisper in the breeze.
We'll keep one ancient village just to show
What England once was when the times were slow—
Broadway for me. But here I know I must
Ask the opinion of our National Trust.
And ev'ry old cathedral that you enter
By then will be an Area Culture Centre.
Instead of nonsense about Death and Heaven
Lectures on civic duty will be given;
Eurhythmic classes dancing round the spire,
And economics courses in the choir.
So don't encourage tourists. Stay your hand
Until we've really got the country plann'd.'

Huxley Hall

In the Garden City Café with its murals on the wall
Before a talk on 'Sex and Civics' I meditated on the Fall.

Deep depression settled on me under that electric glare
While outside the lightsome poplars flanked the rose-beds in
    the square.

While outside the carefree children sported in the summer haze
And released their inhibitions in a hundred different ways.

She who eats her greasy crumpets snugly in the inglenook
Of some birch-enshrouded homestead, dropping butter on her
    book

Can she know the deep depression of this bright, hygienic hell?
And her husband, stout free-thinker, can he share in it as well?

Not the folk-museum's charting of man's Progress out of slime
Can release me from the painful seeming accident of Time.

Barry smashes Shirley's dolly, Shirley's eyes are crossed with
    hate,
Comrades plot a Comrade's downfall 'in the interests of the
    State'.

Not my vegetarian dinner, not my lime-juice minus gin,
Quite can drown a faint conviction that we may be born in
    Sin.

Chelsea 1977

The street is bathed in winter sunset pink,
The air is redolent of kitchen sink,
Between the dog-mess heaps I pick my way
To watch the dying embers of the day
Glow over Chelsea, crimson load on load
All Brangwynesque[1] across the long King's Road.
Deep in myself I feel a sense of doom,
Fearful of death I trudge towards the tomb.
The earth beneath my feet is hardly soil
But outstretched chicken-netting coil on coil
Cover cables, sewage-pipes and wires
While underneath burn hell's eternal fires.
Snap! crackle! pop! The kiddiz know the sound
And Satan stokes his furnace underground.

---

[1] Sir Frank Brangwyn (1867–1956), Welsh painter and pupil of William Morris, known for the realism and intense colours of his murals.

Slough

Come, friendly bombs, and fall on Slough
It isn't fit for humans now,
There isn't grass to graze a cow
   Swarm over, Death!

Come, bombs, and blow to smithereens
Those air-conditioned, bright canteens,
Tinned fruit, tinned meat, tinned milk, tinned beans
   Tinned minds, tinned breath.

Mess up the mess they call a town—
A house for ninety-seven down
And once a week a half-a-crown
   For twenty years,

And get that man with double chin
Who'll always cheat and always win,
Who washes his repulsive skin
   In women's tears,

And smash his desk of polished oak
And smash his hands so used to stroke
And stop his boring dirty joke
   And make him yell.

But spare the bald young clerks who add
The profits of the stinking cad;
It's not their fault that they are mad,
   They've tasted Hell.

It's not their fault they do not know
The birdsong from the radio,
It's not their fault they often go
    To Maidenhead

And talk of sports and makes of cars
In various bogus Tudor bars
And daren't look up and see the stars
    But belch instead.

In labour-saving homes, with care
Their wives frizz out peroxide hair
And dry it in synthetic air
    And paint their nails.

Come, friendly bombs, and fall on Slough
To get it ready for the plough.
The cabbages are coming now;
    The earth exhales.

7

The Ecumenical Church

7 The Ecumenical Church

John Betjeman's passion for the Church of England did not preclude his interest in the wider Church, not to mention some more obscure fringe movements. For a time in the 1930s Betjeman worshipped with the Society of Friends, many of his close friends were Roman Catholic and his mother, like others of her generation, had dabbled on the fringes in Christian Science. His teddy bear Archie was a Strict Baptist.[1] Betjeman's several poems on various manifestations of Christianity are worth examining together. The first three of these represent variants of low church dissent, sects of Christian worship that the poet cannot quite understand or respect. The next four poems touch on aspects of liturgical churches, namely the three branches of Christianity that embrace the doctrine of apostolic succession within the episcopate. His treatment here of the Orthodox, Anglican and Catholic churches is not surprisingly more reverent and serious. However, it is noteworthy that even in these poems – except the last, which is Betjeman's saddest and most personal poem – he maintains his humour.

'An Eighteenth-Century Calvinistic Hymn' is perhaps the most irreverent of the bunch. This poem, built on the humorous effect of an anapestic rhythm, satirizes the Calvinist's tendency toward a masochistic spirituality. The Calvinist denies himself every pleasure except the pleasure he takes in his physical and

---

[1] See Betjeman, *Archie and the Strict Baptists* for a fuller account of the bear's life and religious observance.

mental pain. Anticipating an eternal reward is possible only by focusing on his bodily agony, and by exaggerating his present suffering the Calvinist can more easily convince himself and others of his spiritual worthiness. In such a formula, body and spirit are so dichotomized that the condition of one is interpreted as the binary of the other.

'Undenominational' describes an evangelical revival of emotional fervour. By placing himself near the action, Betjeman can reflect on this sort of religious experience more personally. This is not to say that the poem avoids humour. Instead of describing the vigour and joy that generally characterizes the hymn-singing of such congregations, Betjeman finds amusement in a metrical arrangement of the titles of the hymn-tunes the gathered worshippers are belting out. Despite his effort to distance himself emotionally from the revival, the speaker's proximity to the 'conventicle' encourages a degree of involvement and even self-examination. Though at first he feels rather smug and superior to the congregation and its minister, he comes to sense that such a faith can be 'A beacon in the dark', a light of truth to guide one along the spiritual journey. Although this thought refreshes his spirit, he does not join the service. He is left with a sensation of spiritual glory but is unconnected to the community of belief.

'The Sandemanian Meeting-House in Highbury Quadrant' is inspired by a little-known Scottish sect that blossomed in the nineteenth century. The Sandemanians, also known as Glassites, adhered to a literal reading of Scripture and so minimized contact with the secular world that they did not even actively pursue new converts to their faith. The typical Sunday service lasted all day, being divided by a 'Love Feast' to which Betjeman alludes in his poem. The aspect of the Sandemanians that Betjeman dwells on is their obscurity. Their meeting house is at a busy London junction; few people even notice it or the worshippers, and fewer still know what goes on behind the 'fast-shut' door. For Betjeman there is a mix of respect and amusement: respect for their quiet devotion and isolation from a sinful world, but amusement at what he imagines of their services, 'the barks and the shouts and the greetings'. While the poem condescends, it is refreshingly honest about human nature. This poem really tells us nothing of the Sandemanians; instead it reminds us of our natural instinct to find amusement in that which we do not understand.

'Greek Orthodox' contrasts the ancient and vital Orthodox Church with an Anglicanism that is both divisive and hidebound. The speaker is a type of that breed of Englishmen formed by a traditional public school education. He has gone to Greece to see the ancient sites described in his sixth-form texts, but when he arrives he finds himself drawn to a church. Captivated by its icons and their portrayals of ancient persecutions, the speaker considers the faith of the Greek people and the astonishing hold the Church has over its people. This is an old faith, but one vibrantly alive. It is a tree rooted 'in pre-Christian mud', but it has grown steadily by the fertilizing sacrifices of Christian martyrs. Unlike the Church of England with all its divisions and conflicts, the Orthodox seem untroubled by theological or liturgical controversy. Illustrating the admirable unity of the Orthodox, the poet describes an entire village gathered together for Mass; in this gathering is a serenity that transcends social boundaries, joining all Greeks together in the single, vital purpose of worshipping God.

'Anglo-Catholic Congresses' is about the burgeoning of high church Anglicanism after the Oxford Movement. By the twentieth century, the Church of England had itself become broader in its various liturgical manifestations. This poem captures the voice of an aging poet remembering with excitement his youthful discovery of the beauty and pageantry of Anglo-Catholicism: the incense, the bells, the vestments, the candles, the processions and so forth. Betjeman, who in 1927 attended the Third Congress, recalls the sense of triumph as the movement swept across the Church; while many Church leaders were restoring Anglicanism to the historic, Catholic liturgical tradition, those with low church and evangelical leanings feared that it was moving toward popery. The poem concludes with a picture of a Church dealing with so much more than the aesthetics of worship and the ensuing conflicts; Betjeman has witnessed in this movement a revitalization of faith and a rebirth of devotion, 'the waking days / When Faith was taught and fanned to a golden blaze.'

'An Ecumenical Invitation' is a dramatic monologue in which the speaker, a woman and a Roman Catholic, has invited Betjeman to speak before the Catholic League of Women Journalists. The poem is mostly satirical in its portrayal of the Catholic mind. Betjeman's first appeal is to the stereotype of Catholic reproductive habits – the speaker has ten children. But his primary target is his perception that Catholics view Anglicans and Protestants with a smug sense of spiritual superiority. For instance, the speaker claims to disavow the Catholic use of the term 'non-Catholic' for other Christians yet utters it anyway because she cannot think of another term to use, and then she further undermines the ecumenical dialogue by inadvertently referring to Betjeman as a 'rank outsider'. To him this indicates an unwillingness on the part of Catholics to see other Christians as being part of the Church. The poem's title is ironic, for ecumenical dialogue is difficult when one group sees other believers as simply 'not us'. Moreover, the speaker cannot resist the urge to gloat about differences in church attendance. Anglican cathedrals may be beautiful but they are empty; Roman cathedrals may be 'brash and cheap' but are always full of worshippers. In fact she patronizingly pities both Anglican and Roman, requesting of Betjeman that the Church of England complete its Anglo-Catholic metamorphosis by returning its churches to the Holy Father, the rightful owner dispossessed of his ecclesial property since the sixteenth century. As in Browning's dramatic monologues, the speaker in 'An Ecumenical Invitation' reveals more about herself and her attitudes than she is ever of aware of.

Betjeman's somewhat antagonistic attitude to the Roman faith was personal. He wrote 'The Empty Pew' in 1948 after his wife Penelope was received into the Roman Catholic Church. He was hurt deeply by what he perceived to be an abandonment, and in part he blamed Evelyn Waugh, who had for months harangued both of them as apostate Anglicans who could be saved from the flames of hell only by embracing the true Catholic faith. 'The Empty Pew' describes Betjeman's initial pain of attending his church alone, of seeing the empty pew, and imagining her prayers for him in her new church. The irritation of being prayed for as a heretic was not nearly so searing as the pain of his loneliness, but the poem emphasizes the power of God's love to heal him of his suffering, even if it takes an eternity. He wrote this poem as a sonnet, the form appropriate to the tradition of a yearning lover, and indeed in this poem he mourns as for a lost love. Perhaps not surprisingly, he portrays his passion in a deeply religious demeanour.

This last poem reveals what many of his poems reveal: that no matter what the subject of his poem, Betjeman's perspective is always profoundly spiritual. He is a poet who imbues each human emotion and experience with a religious sensibility. It is Betjeman's Anglican perspective that best defines him as a poet.

An Eighteenth-Century Calvinistic Hymn

Thank God my Afflictions are such
　　That I cannot lie down on my Bed,
And if I but take to my Couch
　　I incessantly Vomit and Bleed.

I am not too sure of my Worth,
　　Indeed it is tall as a Palm;
But what Fruits can it ever bring forth
　　When Leprosy sits at the Helm?

Though Torment's the Soul's Goal's Rewards
　　The contrary's Proof of my Guilt,
While Dancing, Backgammon and Cards,
　　Are among the worst Symptoms I've felt.

Oh! I bless the good Lord for my Boils
　　For my mental and bodily pains,
For without them my Faith all congeals
　　And I'm doomed to HELL'S NE'ER-ENDING
　　FLAMES.

Undenominational

Undenominational
    But still the church of God
He stood in his conventicle
    And ruled it with a rod.

Undenominational
    The walls around him rose,
The lamps within their brackets shook
    To hear the hymns he chose.

'Glory' 'Gopsal' 'Russell Place'
    'Wrestling Jacob' 'Rock'
'Saffron Walden' 'Safe at Home'
    'Dorking' 'Plymouth Dock'[1]

I slipped about the chalky lane
    That runs without the park,
I saw the lone conventicle
    A beacon in the dark.

Revival ran along the hedge
    And made my spirit whole
When steam was on the window panes
    And glory in my soul.

---

[1] Hymns, given by their tune titles, associated with the evangelical movement.

The Sandemanian[1] Meeting-House in Highbury Quadrant

On roaring iron down the Holloway Road
    The red trams and the brown trams pour,
And little each yellow-faced jolted load
    Knows of the fast-shut grained oak door.

From Canonbury, Dalston and Mildmay Park
    The old North London shoots in a train
To the long black platform, gaslit and dark,
    Oh Highbury Station once and again.

Steam or electric, little they care,
    Yellow brick terrace or terracotta hall,
White-wood sweet shop or silent square,
    That the LORD OF THE SCRIPTURES IS LORD
        OF ALL.

Away from the barks and the shouts and the greetings,
    Psalm-singing over and love-lunch done,
Listening to the Bible in their room for meetings,
    Old Sandemanians are hidden from the sun.

---

[1] Religious sect developed by Robert Sandeman (1718–71) from the Glasites.

Greek Orthodox

What did I see when first I went to Greece?
Shades of the Sixth across the Peloponnese.
Though clear the clean-cut Doric temple shone
Still droned the voice of Mr Gidney[1] on;
'That ὅτι? Can we take its meaning here
Wholly as interrogative?' Edward Lear,[2]
Show me the Greece of wrinkled olive boughs
Above red earth; thin goats, instead of cows,
Each with its bell; the shallow terraced soil;
The stone-built wayside shrine; the yellow oil;
The tiled and cross-shaped church, who knows how
          old
Its ashlar walls of honey-coloured gold?
Three centuries or ten? Of course, there'll be
The long meander off to find the key.

The domed interior swallows up the day.
Here, where to light a candle is to pray,
The candle flame shows up the almond eyes
Of local saints who view with no surprise
Their martyrdoms depicted upon walls
On which the filtered daylight faintly falls.
The flame shows up the cracked paint—sea-green blue
And red and gold, with grained wood showing
          through—

---

[1] A.R. Gidney was Betjeman's Greek master in his lower sixth-form at Marlborough. Betjeman never forgave Gidney for his many cruelties to him.
[2] Edward Lear (1812–88), though famous today for his nonsense verse, was widely known in his own time for his paintings and his travels. He visited Greece numerous times, painting popular scenes in oil. As a child, Betjeman purchased a folio of Lear's lithographs of the Ionian isles.

Of much-kissed ikons, dating from, perhaps,
The fourteenth century. There across the apse,
Ikon- and oleograph-adorned, is seen
The semblance of an English chancel screen.

'With *oleographs*?' you say. 'Oh, what a pity!
Surely the diocese has some committee
Advising it on taste?' It is not so.
Thus vigorously does the old tree grow,
By persecution pruned, watered with blood,
Its living roots deep in pre-Christian mud,
It needs no bureaucratical protection.
It is its own perpetual resurrection.
Or take the galleon metaphor—it rides
Serenely over controversial tides
Triumphant to the Port of Heaven, its home,
With one sail missing—that's the Pope's in Rome.

Vicar, I hope it will not be a shock
To find this village has no 'eight o'clock'.
Those bells you heard at eight were being rung
For matins of a sort but matins sung.
Soon will another set of bells begin
And all the villagers come crowding in.
The painted boats rock empty by the quay
Feet crunch on gravel, faintly beats the sea.
From the domed church, as from the sky, look down
The Pantocrator's[1] searching eyes of brown,
With one serene all-comprehending stare
On farmer, fisherman and millionaire.

---

[1] In Byzantine and Hellenic art, the Almighty, either Christ or God.

Anglo-Catholic Congresses[1]

We, who remember the Faith, the grey-headed ones,
　Of those Anglo-Catholic Congresses swinging along,
Who heard the South Coast salvo of incense-guns
　And surged to the Albert Hall in our thousands strong
　With 'extreme' colonial bishops leading in song;

We, who remember, look back to the blossoming May-time
　On ghosts of servers and thurifers after Mass,
The slapping of backs, the flapping of cassocks, the play-time,
　A game of Grandmother's Steps on the vicarage grass—
　'Father, a little more sherry. I'll fill your glass.'

We recall the triumph, that Sunday after Ascension,
　When our Protestant suffragan suffered himself to be coped—
The SYA and the Scheme for Church Extension—
　The new diocesan's not as 'sound' as we'd hoped,
　And Kensit[2] threatens and has Sam Gurney[3] poped?

Yet, under the Travers[4] baroque, in a limewashed whiteness,
　The fiddle-back vestments a-glitter with morning rays,
Our Lady's image, in multiple-candled brightness,
　The bells and banners—those were the waking days
　When Faith was taught and fanned to a golden blaze.

---

[1] In the 1920s, these meetings foregrounded Anglo-Catholicism in the life of the
　Church of England.
[2] John Kensit (1853–1902) and his son John Alfred Kensit (1881–1957) were militant
　protestants and vigorous opponents of Anglo-Catholicism.
[3] Samuel Gurney (1885–1968) was a friend and neighbour of Betjeman's. He was a
　devotee of Anglo-Catholicism and restorer of churches. ('To pope' is to become a
　Roman Catholic.)
[4] Martin Travers (1896–1948) was the designer of many Anglo-Catholic church
　interiors.

An Ecumenical Invitation

This is my tenth; his name is Damien—
Not Damien of Braganza, on whose day
My second youngest, Catherine, was born
(Antonia Fraser[1] is her godmamma),
But Damien after Father Damien,
Whom Holy Church has just beatified.
But I forget, you're not a Catholic,
And this will seem too technical to you.
Still, never mind, there's whisky over there,
Gin, sherry—help yourself—no, not for me.
     Teresa, please take Damien away
I want to talk to Mr Betjeman.
     Well, tell me what you think of the reforms.
I understand that *you* have had some too,
Isn't *The Times* improved beyond belief?[2]
It's so much bigger than it used to be!
I never like that term 'non-Catholic'—
The word we used to use for Anglicans,
Though several of my really greatest friends
Were once non-Catholics—take Evelyn Waugh[3]
(God rest his soul!) and Graham Sutherland;[4]
And quite the sweetest girl I ever knew,
A district nurse, was once a Methodist—
But oh, so happy as a Catholic now.
Now, won't you give our churches back to us?

---

[1] Antonia Fraser (1932–), novelist and historian, was the daughter of Frank and Elizabeth Pakenham (Lord and Lady Longford). Betjeman knew her father and uncle well and corresponded with both.
[2] William Rees-Mogg (1928–), a Roman Catholic, was Editor of *The Times* from 1967–81.
[3] Evelyn Waugh (1903–66), novelist, was a friend of Betjeman and his wife Penelope.
[4] Graham Sutherland (1903–80) was a well-known artist and portrait painter.

Then you'll be Catholics too! I realise
It's somehow all mixed up with politics,
The Holy Father, though, will see to that;
What was I saying? England's heritage—
It *does* seem such a pity, doesn't it?
Those fine cathedrals crumbling to decay
Half empty, while our own, though brash and cheap,
Are always, always, crowded to the doors.
    But still I didn't ask you here for that,
I want to speak of something near my heart—
The Catholic League of Women Journalists.
I, for my sins, am President this year
And with ecumenism in the air
I thought—you'll know the Holy Father's said
That all the Christians in the world, the rank
Outsiders, I mean those outside our ranks,
As well as Catholics, must play their part,
And that was why I thought of asking you
To give us this year's annual address.
It's quite informal, only half an hour.

The Empty Pew[1]

In the perspective of Eternity
  The pain is nothing, now you go away
  Above the steaming thatch how silver-grey
Our chiming church tower, calling 'Come to me

My Sunday-sleeping villagers!' And she,
  Still half my life, kneels now with those who say
  'Take courage, daughter. Never cease to pray
God's grace will break him of his heresy.'

I, present with our Church of England few
  At the dear words of Consecration see
  The chalice lifted, hear the sanctus chime
And glance across to that deserted pew.
  In the Perspective of Eternity
  The pain is nothing—but, ah God, in Time.

[1] Although written in 1948 when Penelope Betjeman was received into the Roman Catholic Church, it was not published until after the deaths of both John and Penelope Betjeman.